P V

❦ Breuissima rela
cion de la destruycion de las In-
dias:colegida por el Obispo dō
fray Bartolome de las Casas/o
Casaus de la orden de Sācto Do
mingo.
Año. 1552.

Illustration 1: Original cover of the first manuscript of A Brief Account of the Destruction of the Indies. 1552.

A Brief Account of the Destruction of the Indies

Colegida por el Obispo don

Friar Bartolomé de las Casas

o Casaus de la Órden de Sacto Domingo. Año 1552.

Audiobook source: Libri Vox.
The vector for the audiobook image was created by roseodionova.

ISBN: 9781705585979
Printing: Published Independently

Front: De Bry, Theodor, ca. 1598. Dismemberment of infant to feed dogs. Illustration on Brevíssima relación de la destrucción de las Indias. Frankfurt, 1598.

TABLE OF CONTENTS

ILLUSTRATIONS

ABOUT THIS BOOK

Brief Account of the Destruction of the Indies tells the extreme cruelty with which the conquerors treated Indians in America, which contributed to the disappearance of great civilizations. The work was written by Bartolomé de las Casas, a former conqueror and Dominican friar that influenced the public policy for the Indies. The book is a primary source of historical data, told by someone who witnessed some of the events in the story. It was first published in 1552, sixty years after the discovery of America, to alert the future King Philip II about the injustices that were committed against the natives. After this work was published, a complete reform of the Indian legislation was carried out and "New Laws" were promulgated. One of the main purposes of the new legislation was the abolition of Indian slavery and the *commissions[1]* regime that gave rise to ill-treatment and injustices against the Indians. In Europe, this book was a symbol of the era of fanaticism and intolerance of men, fostering an anti-Spanish feeling that was already brewing. Some detractors of Friar de las Casas argued that the information about the excesses committed by the colonizers was exaggerated. However, time has given Friar de las Casas the reason. There is evidence that some of his writings coincide with the story told by indigenous tribes.

Audiovisual Resources

The book includes illustrations by Theodor de Bry, which were published in the 1558 edition, for which we have included links to modern versions that incorporate three-dimensional technology.

Each chapter of the book gives the reader the opportunity to read the content or listen to it in audiobook format. The audiobook was produced by Librivox, a digital library with public domain content. On the digital version

---

[1] The commission, or "encomienda," was an institution implemented by the Spanish conquerors during the colonization of America, to take advantage of indigenous labor. It consisted of delivering a group of Indians to a Spaniard so that he could protect, educate and evangelize them. Indians had to pay a tribute as an obligation of "vassals" of the Crown, thus rewarding the services provided by the "encomendero".

of this book, the access to the audio files is provided through an icon placed at the beginning of each chapter.

Readers using the traditional format can access the audiobook through the following address:

http://bit.ly/brief-casas

Illustration 2: Unknown author. Friar Bartolomé de las Casas accompanied by Indians and settlers [engraving].

FRIAR BARTOLOMÉ DE LAS CASAS

Friar Bartolomé de las Casas was born in Seville in 1474 and died in Madrid in 1566. He was a Spanish chronicler who defended the rights of the Indians during the beginning of the colonization of America. De las Casas arrived in the Indies in 1502, ten years after the discovery of America, as part of the expedition of Nicolás de Ovando, the new governor of the Indies. In 1506, he received a commission in Hispaniola, after having fought against the Taíno Indians. Two years later, he was ordained a priest and thereafter he combined the priesthood with the office of the commissioner[2]. Years later he participated in the conquest of Cuba and

---

[2] The commissioner or *encomendero*, was a Spanish conqueror that was assigned an *encomienda* (as per in footnote number. 1).

performed intermediary tasks with the Indians. For this, he was awarded a distribution of Indians, and worked in the exploration of gold deposits.

Distressed by the abuses of the Spanish settlers towards the Indians, Friar Bartolomé de las Casas undertook a campaign to defend their human rights and began by renouncing the commission he had been granted in Cuba. In 1515, he moved to Seville to tell the authorities about his experiences and the abuses committed on the Indians. During this time, de las Casas promoted a more agricultural than mining colonial economy, reinforced by the importation of African black slaves. In 1516, King Charles appointed him Universal Protector of the Indians.

In 1520, de las Casas tried to create a peaceful colony in Cumana to show that Indians and Spaniards could live in harmony but failed. In 1537, he led another colonization company in Guatemala, this time with more success, since he obtained control of the territory by peaceful means and banished the practice of the *commissions*.

In 1540 he returned to Spain to expose King Charles I to his demands and complaints about the treatment he continued to give to the Indians. In 1543, de las Casas was appointed Bishop of Chiapas (Mexico), but his parishioners reacted hostile to his rigorous moral demands and he had to return to Spain.

From 1551 until his death, de las Casas was "Procurador de Indios," (the "Indian Ombudsman") whose responsibilities included the notification of complaints received from the indigenous population of the entire Americas. In 1552, de las Casas published the Short Account of the Destruction of the Indies, a work that denounces the atrocities committed by the Spaniards in the New World since the beginning of the conquest and throughout the colonization. De las Casas dedicated this work to Phillip II, who was in charge of Indian affairs after the death of his father Charles V. The publication of this book had a devastating effect on Spain. Multiple editions, in multiple languages, were published throughout Europe, paying for the negative image of the Spaniards, and the cruel nature of the Pope.

PREFACE

Presentation by Bishop don Friar Bartolomé de las Casas, or Casaus to the mist high and potent lord Prince of all the Spains don Felipe, our lord.

Most high and potent lord:

Because divine providence has ordered in this world that for the direction and common utility of the human lineage the world be constituted by Kingdoms and peoples, with their kings like fathers and shepherds (as Homer has called them) and therefore the most noble and generous members of the republics, for that reason no doubt of the rectitude of the royal spirits of those kings may be held, or with right reason might be held. And if any wrongs, failings, defects, or evils should be suffered in those kingdoms, the only reason for that is that the kings have no notice of them. For these wrongs &c, if they be present and reported, it is the duty of the King, with greatest study and vigilant industry to root them out. This appears to have been the meaning of divine scripture in the proverbs of Solomon: *Rex qui sedet in solio iudicii, dissipat omne malum intuitio suo*[3]. For its clear that with the innate and natural virtue of the king, the mere notice of wrong or malefaction in his kingdom more than suffices for him to scatter it, and should such ills arise, not for a single moment could he tolerate them.

Considering then, most potent lord, the evils and harm, the perditions and ruin – the equals or likes of which, never where men imagined capable of doing – considering, as I say, those evils which as a land of 50 years and more experience, being in those lands present, I have seen committed upon those so many and such great kingdoms, or better said, that entire vast and Ne World of the Indies – and conceded and given in trust by God and His Church to the King and queen of Castile, to rue and govern them, convert them to belief in Christ and the Holy Catholic Church, and give them to prosper temporally and spiritually - , this subject was not able to contain himself from supplicating with Your Majesty, most importunely, that Your

---

[3] The king, that sitteth on the throne of judgment, scattereth away all evil with his look.

5

Majesty not concede such license nor allow those terrible things that the tyrants did invent, pursue and have committed against those peaceable, humble, and meek Indian peoples, who offend no person. For these are things that are iniquitous tyrannous, and condemned, detested and accursed by all natural, divine, and human law (though they be called "conquests"), yet which, if they be allowed, those evil men shall, most surely, commit once more. Considering, then, the perditions of infinite souls and bodies that those subjects had once perpetrated bad would again, I, not being a prisoner rendered mute, deliberated to put into writing so that Your Highness might more easily read them, some – a very few – examples that in days past I had collected from among the countless numbers that I could in truth declare.

An as the Archbishop of Toledo, teacher of Your Highness, was Bishop of Your Highness, was Bishop of Cartagena, he did ask that account of me and presented it to Your Highness, but because of the long paths of sea and land that your Highness has traveled and the frequent royal occupations Your Highness had, it may be that either Your Highness did not read that account or has forgotten that Your Highness has it. And yet such is the temerity and unreasonable eagerness of those who think nothing of spilling such immense quantities of human blood and depopulating those vast lands of their natural inhabitants and possessors, killing a thousand million souls and stealing incomparable treasures, that it grows stronger every day, and so by diverse paths and several feigned colors these tyrannical men importune that they be conceded or allowed said conquests (which cannot be conceded to them without violation of natural and divine law, and therefore commission of most grave mortal sins, worthy of terrible, eternal moments). Thus, I though it right to serve Your Highness with this brief and abbreviated summary of that otherwise voluminous narration of the devastations and perditions which might be, and ought to be, composed. I beg that Your Highness read it with the generosity and royal benignity that is Your Highness wont with the works of those subjects and servants of thine who desire to serve purely and solely to further the public weal and the prosperity of the royal estate. And once your Highness has seen the deformity of the injustice which upon those innocent people is done, destroying them and cutting them to pieces without cause or just reason for it, but rather out of mere covetousness and ambition of those who pretend to do such nefarious deeds – once this deformity has been seen, I say, and has been understood, I beg that Your Highness be kind enough to supplicate and persuade His

6

Majesty to deny any man who might propose to undertake such noxious and detestable enterprises, and instead lay perpetual silence upon that infernal request, with such fear and terror that no man might thereafter dare even so much as name it.

This is a thing, my most high Lord, which is most sorely needful and necessary so that God might make the entire estate of the royal crown of Castile prosper spiritually and temporally and preserve it and bestow upon its blessings. Amen.

Illustration 3: Author and date unknown. La Santa María, main ship of Christopher Columbus, accompanied by La Niña and La Pinta [wood engraving]. 3D image on **http://bit.ly/lascasas3***.*

A SHORT ACCOUNT OF THE DESTRUCTION OF THE INDIES

http://bit.ly/bre-brief

America was discovered and found out *Ann. Dom.* 1492, and the year ensuing inhabited by the Spaniards, and afterward a multitude of them travelled thither[4] from Spain for the space of nine and forty years. Their first attempt was on the Hispaniola island, which indeed is a most fertile soil, and at present in great reputation for its spaciousness and length, containing in circumference six hundred leagues[5]. Nay it is on all sides surrounded with an almost innumerable number of islands, which we found so well peopled with natives and foreigners, that there is scarce any region in the universe fortified with so many inhabitants. But the mainland or continent, distant from this island two hundred and fifty leagues and upwards, extends itself above ten thousand leagues in length near the seashore, which lands are some of them already discovered, and more may be found out in process of time. And such a multitude of people inhabits these countries, that it seems as if the Omnipotent God has assembled and convocated the major part of mankind in this part of the World.

Now this infinite multitude of men are by the creation of God innocently simple, altogether void of and averse to all manner of craft, subtlety and malice, and most obedient and loyal subjects to their native sovereigns; and behave themselves very patiently, submissively and quietly towards the Spaniards, to whom they are subservient and subject; so that finally they live without the least thirst after revenge, laying aside all litigiousness, commotion and hatred. All these universes and infinite people, God raised simplest, without evils or folds, very obedient, very faithful to their natural lords and to the Christians they serve; humbler, more patient, more peaceful and still, without quarrels or bustles, not ruthless, not cuddly, without resentment, without hatred, without wanting revenge, which is in the world. They are

---

[4] Archaic, "toward the place."

[5] A Spanish league (*legua*) is about 2.6 miles. A day's journey on horseback was often calculated as seven *leguas*.

likewise the most delicate, skinny and tender people in complexion and that less can suffer jobs, and that more easily die of any disease. Neither children of princes and lords among us, raised in gifts and delicate life are not more delicate than them, even if they are among those who are of lineage of farmers. This nation is very necessitous and indigent, masters of very slender possessions, and consequently, neither haughty, nor ambitious. They are parsimonious in their diet, as the holy fathers were in their frugal life in the desert, known by the name of *eremites*. Indians are mostly naked, and at the most, they wear a type of cotton blanket measuring one or two and a half *varas*[6]. They lie on a coarse rug or matt, and those that have the most plentiful estate or fortunes, the better sort, use network, knotted at the four corners in lieu of beds, which the inhabitants of the island of *Hispaniola*, in their own proper idiom, term *hamacas*[7]. The men are pregnant and docile. The natives tractable, and capable of morality or goodness, very apt to receive the instilled principles of Catholic religion; nor are they averse to civility and good manners, being not so much discomposed by variety of obstructions, as the rest of mankind; insomuch, that having sucked in (if I may so express myself) the very first rudiments of the Christian Faith, they are so transported with zeal and fervor in the exercise of ecclesiastical sacraments, and divine service, that the very religious themselves, stand in need of the greatest and most signal patience to undergo such extreme transports. And to conclude, I myself have heard the Spaniards themselves (who dare not assume the confidence to deny the good nature predominant in them) declare, that there was nothing wanting in them for the acquisition of eternal beatitude, but the sole knowledge and understanding of the deity.

The Spaniards first assaulted the innocent sheep, so qualified by the Almighty, as is aforementioned, like most cruel tigers, wolves and lions' hunger-starved, studying nothing, for the space of forty years, after their first landing. But the massacre of these wretches, whom they have so inhumanely and barbarously butchered and harassed with several kinds of torments, never before known, or heard (of which you shall have some account in the

---

[6] A *vara* measures about .8 meters

[7] Hammock, this is one of many Taíno words adopted by Spaniards. Other terms derived from the Taíno language include hurricane (in Spanish, *huracán*), barbecue (*barbacoa*), yucca (*yuca*), iguana, maize (*maíz*), and tabacco (*tabaco*).

following discourse) that of three millions of persons, which lived in Hispaniola itself, there is at present but the inconsiderable remnant of scarce three hundred.

The Isle of Cuba, which extends as far, as Valladolid in Spain is distant from Rome, lies now uncultivated, like a desert, and interred in its own ruins. You may also find the Isles of San Juan[8], and Jamaica, both large and fruitful places, unpeopled and desolate. The Lucayan Islands on the North Side, adjacent to Hispaniola and Cuba, which are sixty in number, or thereabout, together with those, vulgarly known by the name of the Gigantic Isles, and others, the most infertile whereof, exceeds the royal garden of Sevilla in fruitfulness, a most healthful and pleasant climate is now laid waste and uninhabited. Whereas, when the Spaniards first arrived here, about 500,000 souls dwelt in it, they are now cut off, some by slaughter, and others ravished away by force and violence, to work in the mines of Hispaniola, which was destitute of native inhabitants: For a certain vessel, sailing to this Isle, to the end, that the harvest being over (some good Christian, moved with piety and pity, undertook this dangerous voyage, to convert souls to Christianity) the remaining gleanings might be gathered up, there were only found eleven persons, which I saw with my own eyes. There are other islands thirty in number, and upward bordering upon the isle of San Juan, totally unpeopled; all which are above two thousand leagues in length, and yet remain without inhabitants, native, or people.

As to the firm land, we are certainly satisfied, and assured, that the Spaniards by their barbarous and execrable actions have absolutely depopulated ten kingdoms, of greater extent than all Spain, together with the kingdoms of Aragon and Portugal, that is to say, above one thousand leagues, which now lye vast and desolate, and are absolutely ruined, when as formerly no other country whatsoever was more populous. Nay we dare boldly affirm, that during the forty years' space, wherein they exercised their sanguinary and detestable tyranny in these regions, above twelve million (computing men, women, and children) have undeservedly perished; nor do I conceive that I should deviate from the truth by saying that above fifty million in all paid their last debt to nature.

---

[8] San Juan is the former name of Puerto Rico.

Those that arrived at these islands from the remotest parts of Spain, and who pride themselves in the name of Christians, steered two courses principally, in order to the extirpation, and exterminating of this people from the face of the earth. The first whereof was raising an unjust, sanguinolent, cruel war. The other, by putting them to death, who hitherto, thirsted after their liberty, or designed (which the most potent, strenuous and magnanimous spirits intended) to recover their pristine freedom, and shake off the shackles of so injurious a captivity. For they being taken off in war, none but women and children were permitted to enjoy the benefit of that country-air, in whom they did in succeeding times lay such a heavy work, that the very brutes were more happy than they: To which two species of tyranny as sub-alternate things to the genus, the other innumerable courses they took to extirpate and make this a desolate people, may be reduced and referred.

Now the ultimate end and scope that incited the Spaniards to endeavor the extirpation and desolation of this people, was gold only; that thereby growing opulent in a short time, they might arrive at once at such degrees and dignities, as were no ways consistent with their persons.

Finally, in one word, their ambition and avarice, than which the heart of man never entertained greater, and the vast wealth of those regions; the humility and patience of the inhabitants (which made their approach to these lands more easier) did much promote the business: whom they so despicably contemned, that they treated them (I speak of things which I was an eye witness of, without the least fallacy) not as beasts, which I cordially wished they would, but as the most abject dung and filth of the earth; and so solicitous they were of their life and soul, that the above-mentioned number of people died without understanding the true faith or sacraments. And this also is as really true as the precedent narration (which the very tyrants and cruel murderers cannot deny without the stigma of a lye) that the Spaniards never received any injury from the Indians, but that they rather reverenced them as persons descended from heaven, until that they were compelled to take up arms, provoked thereunto by repeated injuries, violent torments, and unjust butcheries.

OF THE ISLAND HISPANIOLA

http://bit.ly/esp-brief

The Hispaniola island, was the first, as we said, where Christians entered and began the great ravages and perditions of these people. This is where they first destroyed and depopulated, beginning Christians to take the women and children to the Indians to serve themselves and to use them badly and to eat their meals that came out of their sweat and work. They were not happy with what the Indians gave them in good faith, according to the faculty that each one had, which is always small because they usually do not have more than what they ordinarily need and do with little work.

What is enough for 3 houses of 10 people each for a month, the Christian eats it and destroys it in a single day. Among these many other forces, violence, and vexations that made them, the Indians began to understand that those men should not have come from heaven. Some hid their meals, others their women and children, others fled to the mountains to get away from people of such a hard and terrible conversation. The Christians gave them slaps and sticks, until they laid hands on the lords of the towns; and this came to such recklessness and shamelessness that the greatest King lord of the whole island, a Christian captain[9] raped his own wife forcibly.

From which time they began to consider by what ways and means they might expel the Spaniards out of their countries, and immediately took up arms. But, good God, what arms, do you imagine? Namely such, both offensive and defensive, as resemble reeds wherewith boys sport with one another, more than manly arms and weapons. Which the Spaniards no sooner perceived, but they, mounted on generous steeds, well weaponed with lances and swords, begin to exercise their bloody butcheries and stratagems, and overrunning their cities and towns, spared no age, or sex, nay not so much as pregnant women, but ripping up their bellies, tore them alive in pieces. They laid wagers among themselves, who should with a sword at

---

[9] Francisco Roldán, of the companions of Cristóbal Colón.

one blow cut, or divide a man in two; or which of them should decollate or behead a man, with the greatest dexterity; nay farther, which should sheath his sword in the bowels of a man with the quickest dispatch and expedition.

They snatched young babies from the mothers' breasts, and then dashed out the brains of those innocents against the rocks; others they cast into rivers scoffing and jeering them, and called upon their bodies when falling with derision, the true testimony of their cruelty, to come to them, and inhumanely exposing others to their merciless swords, together with the mothers that gave them life. They erected certain gibbets, large, but low made, so that their feet almost reached the ground, every one of which was so ordered as to bear thirteen persons in honor and reverence (as they said blasphemously) of our redeemer and his twelve apostles, under which they made a fire to burn them to ashes whilst hanging on them.

Illustration 4: Indiscriminate murder of women, men and infants [engraving]. On: Brevíssima relación de la destrucción de las Indias. Frankfurt, 1598. 3D image on http://bit.ly/lascasas4.

But those they intended to preserve alive, they dismissed, their hands half cut, and still hanging by the skin, to carry their letters missive to those that fly from us and skulk on the mountains, as an exprobation of their flight.

The lords and persons of noble extract were usually exposed to this kind of death; they ordered gridirons[10] to be placed and supported with wooden forks, and putting a small fire under them, these miserable wretches by degrees and with loud shrieks and exquisite torments, at last expired.

Illustration 5: De Bry, Theodor, ca. 1598. Torments made to lords and nobles [engraving]. On: Brevíssima relación de la destruyción de las Indias. Frankfurt, 1598. 3D image on **http://bit.ly/lascasas5***.*

I once saw four or five of their most powerful lords laid on these gridirons, and thereon roasted, and not far off, two or three more over-spread with the same commodity, man's flesh; but the shrill clamors which were heard there being offensive to the captain, by hindering his repose, he commanded them to be strangled with a halter. The executioner (whose

---

[10] *Gridiron* is a cooking utensil of parallel metal bars; used to grill fish or meat.

name and parents at Sevilla are not unknown to me) prohibited the doing of it; but introduced gags into their mouths to prevent the hearing of the noise (he himself making the fire) till that they dyed, when they had been roasted as long as he thought convenient.

I was an eye-witness of these and innumerable number of other cruelties: and because all men, who could lay hold of the opportunity, sought out lurking holes in the mountains, to avoid as dangerous rocks so brutish and barbarous a people, strangers to all goodness, and the extirpaters and adversaries of men, they bred up such fierce hunting dogs as would devour an Indian like a hog, at first sight in less than a moment: Now such kind of slaughters and cruelties as these were committed by the curs, and if at any time it happened, (which was rarely) that the Indians irritated upon a just account destroyed or took away the life of any Spaniard, they promulgated and proclaimed this law among them, that one hundred Indians should die for every individual Spaniard that should be slain.

OF THE KINGDOMS CONTAINED IN HISPANIOLA

http://bit.ly/rei-brief

This Isle of Hispaniola was made up of six of their greatest kingdoms, and as many most puissant kings, to whose empire almost all the other lords, whose number was infinite, did pay their allegiance. One of these kingdoms was called Magua, signifying a campaign or open country; which is very observable, if any place in the universe deserves taking notice of, and memorable for the pleasantness of its situation; for it is extended from South to North eighty leagues, in breadth five, eight, and in some parts ten leagues in length; and is on all sides enclosed with the highest mountains; above thirty thousand rivers, and rivulets water her coasts, twelve of which prodigious number do not yield in all in magnitude to those famous rivers, the Eber, Duer, and Guadalquivir; and all those Rivers which have their source or spring from the mountains lying Westerly, the number whereof is twenty thousand) are very rich in mines of gold; on which mountain lies the province of rich mines, whence the exquisite gold of twenty four carats weight, takes denomination. The King and lord of this kingdom was named Guarionex, who governed within the compass of his dominions so many vassals and potent lords, that every one of them was able to bring into the field sixteen thousand soldiers for the service of Guarionex their supreme lord and sovereign, when summoned thereunto. Some of which I was acquainted with. This was a most obedient prince, endued with great courage and morality, naturally of a pacific temper, and most devoted to the service of the Castilian Kings. This King commanded and ordered his subjects, that every one of those lords under his jurisdiction, should present him with a bell full of gold; but in succeeding times, being unable to perform it, they were commanded to cut it in two, and fill one part therewith, for the inhabitants of this isle were altogether inexperienced, and unskillful in mine-works, and the digging gold out of them. This Cacique[11] proffered his service to the King of Castile, on this condition, that he would take care, that those lands should be cultivated and manured, wherein, during the reign of Isabella, Queen of Castile, the Spaniards first set footing and fixed their residence, extending in length even to Santo Domingo, the space of fifty leagues. For he declared (nor was it a fallacy, but an absolute truth,) that his subjects understood not the practical use of digging in golden mines. To which promises he had readily and voluntarily condescended, to my own certain knowledge, and so by this means, the King would have received the annual revenue of three millions of Spanish castelians, and upward, there being at that very time in that island fifty cities ampler and spacious than Sevilla itself in Spain.

But what returns by way of remuneration and reward did they make this so clement and benign monarch, can you imagine, no other but this? They put the greatest indignity upon him imaginable in the person of his consort who was violated by a Spanish Captain altogether unworthy of the name of Christian. He might indeed probably expect to meet with a convenient time and opportunity of revenging this ignominy so injuriously thrown upon him by preparing military forces to attack him, but he rather chose to abscond in the province De los Ciquayos (wherein a puissant vassal and subject of his ruled) divested of his estate and kingdom, and there live and dye an exile.

---

[11] *Cacique* is a Taíno word used to identify the tribal leader. The term came to be used by conquerors to describe Amerindian chiefs who were believed to be inferior in rank to kings and princesses (*principales*).

But the Spaniards receiving certain information, that he had absented himself, connived no longer at his concealment but raised war against him, who had received them with so great humanity and kindness, and having first laid waste and desolate the whole region, at last found, and took him prisoner, who being bound in fetters was conveyed on board of a ship in order to his transportation to Castile, as a captive: but the vessel perished in the voyage, wherewith many Spaniards were also lost, as well as a great weight of gold, among which there was a prodigious ingot of gold, resembling a large loaf of bread, weighing 3,600 castelians; thus it pleased God to revenge their enormous impieties.

A second kingdom was named Marien[12], where there is to this day a haven, upon the utmost borders of the plain or open country toward the north, more fertile and larger than the kingdom of Portugal; and really deserving constant and frequent inhabitants. For it abounds with mountains, and is rich in mines of gold and *Orichalcum,* a kind of copper metal mixed with gold; The king's name of this place was Guacanagarí, who had many powerful lords (some whereof were not unknown to me) under his subjection. The first that landed in this kingdom when he discovered America was an Admiral[13] well stricken in years, who had so hospitable and kind a reception from the aforesaid Guacanagarí, as well as all those Spaniards that accompanied him in that voyage, giving them all imaginable help and assistance (for the Admiral's vessel[14] was sunk on their coasts) that I heard it from his own mouth, he could not possibly have been entertained with greater caresses and civilities from his own parents in his own native country. But this king, being forced to fly to avoid the Spanish slaughter and cruelty, deprived of all he was master of, died in the mountains; and all the rest of the potentates and nobles, his subjects, perished in that servitude and vassalage; as you shall find in this following treatise.

The third kingdom was distinguished by the appellation of Maguana, another admirable, healthful and fruitful region, where at present the most

---

[12] Bartolomé mentions that there is place called Puerto Real where Marien used to be located.

[13] Cristóbal Colón.

[14] *La Santa María*, which was lost on Christmas Day, 1492.

refined sugar of the island is made. Caonabó then reigned there, who surmounted all the rest in power, state, and the splendid ceremonies of his government. This King beyond all expectation was surprised in his own palace, by the great subtilty and industry of the Spaniards, and after carried on board in order to his transportation to Castile, but there being at that time six ships riding in the haven, and ready to set sail such an impetuous storm suddenly arose, that they as well as the passengers and ship's crew were all lost, together with King Caonabó loaded with irons; by which judgment the almighty declared that this was as unjust and impious an act as any of the former. This Kind had three or four brothers then living, men of strength and valor, who being highly incensed at the captivity of their King and brother, to which he was injuriously reduced, having also intelligence of the devastations and butcheries committed by the Spaniards in other regions, and not long after hearing of their brother's death, took up arms to revenge themselves of the enemy, whom the Spaniards met with, and certain party of horse (which proved very offensive to the Indians) made such havoc and slaughter among them, that the half of this kingdom was laid waste and depopulated.

Xaraguá is the fourth kingdom, and as it were the center and middle of the whole island and is not to be equaled for fluency of speech and politeness of idiom or dialect by any inhabitants of the other kingdoms, and in policy and morality transcends them all. Herein the lords and peers abounded, and the very populace excelled in in stature and habit of body: their King was Behechio by name who had a sister called Anacaona, and both the brother as well as sister had loaded the Spaniards with benefits and singular acts of civility, and by delivering them from the evident and apparent danger of death, did signal services to the Castilian Kings. Behechio dying the supreme power of the kingdom fell to Anacaona: But it happened one day, that the governor[15] of an island, attended by 60 horse, and 30 foot (now the cavalry was sufficiently able to unpeople not only the isle, but also the whole continent) he summoned about 300 dynasts, or noblemen to appear before him, and commanded the most powerful of them, being first crowded into a thatched barn or hovel, to be exposed to the fury of the merciless fire, and

---

[15] Presumably Nicolás de Ovando, who was made governor of the Americas in 1501 and reached Hispaniola in April 1502. Las Casas arrived to las Americas on the same fleet.

the rest to be pierced with lances, and run through with the point of the sword, by a multitude of men. And Anacaona herself who (as we said before,) swayed the imperial scepter, to her greater honor, was hanged on a gibbet. And if it fell out that any person instigated by compassion or covetousness, did entertain any Indian boys and mount them on horses, to prevent their murder, another was appointed to follow them, who ran them through the back or in the hinder parts, and if they chanced to escape death, and fall to the ground, they immediately cut off his legs; and when any of those Indians, that survived these barbarous massacres, betook themselves to an isle eight leagues distant, to escape their butcheries, they were then committed to servitude during life.

The fifth kingdom was Higüey, over whom Queen Higuanamá, a superannuated princess, whom the Spaniards crucified, did preside and govern. The number of those I saw here burnt, and dismembered, and racked with various torments, as well as others, who surviving were enslaved, is infinite. But because so much might be said concerning the assassinations and depopulating of these people, as cannot without great difficulty be published in writing (nor do I conceive that one fragile part of 1,000 that is here contained can be fully displayed). I will only add one remark more of the aforementioned wars. I will aver upon my conscience, that notwithstanding all the above-named injustice, the Indians did not, nor was it in their power to give any greater occasion for the commission of them, no more than a pious religioso living in a regulated monastic life. I add farther, that I really believe, and am satisfied by certain undeniable conjectures, that at the very juncture of time, when all these outrages were committed in this Isle, the Indians were not so much guilty of one single mortal sin of commission against the Spaniards, that might deserve from any man revenge or require satisfaction. And as for those sins, the punishment whereof God hath reserved to himself, as the immoderate desire of revenge, hatred, envy or inward rancor of spirit, to which they might be transported against such capital enemies as the Spaniards were, I judge that very few of them can justly be accused of them; for their impetuosity and vigor I speak experimentally, was inferior to that of children of ten or twelve years of age: and this I can assure you, that the Indians had ever a just cause of raising war against the Spaniards, and the Spaniards on the contrary never raised a just war against them, but what was more injurious and groundless then any undertaken by the worst of tyrants. All which I affirm of all their other transactions and passages in America.

The warlike engagements being over, and the inhabitants all swept away, they divided among themselves the young men, women, and children reserved promiscuously for that purpose, one obtained thirty, another forty, to this man one hundred were disposed, to the other two hundred, and the more one was in favor with the domineering tyrant (which they styled governor) the more he became master of, upon this pretense, and with this proviso, that he should see them instructed in the Catholic religion, when as they themselves to whom they were committed to be taught, and the care of their souls instructed them were, for the major part idiots, cruel, avaricious, infected and stained with all sorts of vices. And this was the great care they had of them, they sent the males to the mines to dig and bring away the gold, which is an intolerable labor; but the women they made use of manure and till the ground, which is a toil most irksome even to men of the strongest and most robust constitutions, allowing them no other food but herbage, and such kind of unsubstantial nutriment, so that the nursing women's milk was exsiccated and so dried up, that the young infants lately brought forth, all perished, and females being separated from and debarred cohabitation with men, there was no proliferation or raising up issue among them. The men died in mines, hunger starved and oppressed with labor, and the women perished in the fields, harassed and broken with the like evils and calamities. Thus, an infinite number of inhabitants that formerly peopled this island were exterminated and dwindled away to nothing by such consumptions. They were compelled to carry burthens of eighty or one hundred pound weight, and that an hundred or two hundred leagues complete: and the Spaniards were worn by them on the shoulders in a vehicle or carriage, or kind of beds made of net-work by the Indians; for in truth they made use of them as beasts to carry the burthens and cumbersome baggage of their journeys, insomuch that it frequently happened, that the shoulders and backs of the Indians were deeply marked with their scourges and stripes, just as they used to serve a tired jade, accustomed to burthens. and as to those slashes with whips, blows with staves, cuffs and boxes, maledictions and curses, with a thousand of such kind of torments they suffered during the fatigue of their laborious journeys it would require a long tract of time, and many reams of paper to describe them, and when all were done would only create horror and consternation in the reader.

But here it is observable, that the desolation of these isles and provinces took beginning since the decease of the most serene Queen Isabella[16], about the year 1504, for before that time very few of the provinces situated in that island were oppressed or spoiled with unjust wars, or violated with general devastation as after they were, and most if not all these things were concealed and masked from the Queen's knowledge (whom I hope God hath crowned with eternal glory) for she was transported with fervent and wonderful zeal, nay, almost divine desires for the salvation and preservation of these people, which things so exemplary as these we having seen with our eyes, and felt with our hands, cannot easily be forgotten.

Take this also for a general rule, that the Spaniards upon what American shore they arrived, exercised the same cruelties, slaughters, tyrannies and detestable oppressions on the most innocent Indian nation, and diverting themselves with delights in new sorts of torment, which in time improved in barbarism and cruelty; wherewith the omnipotent being incensed suffered them to fail by a more desperate and dangerous lapse into a reprobate state.

OF THE ISLES OF SAN JUAN AND JAMAICA

 http://bit.ly/san-brief

In the Year 1509, the Spaniards sailed to the islands of San Juan[17] and Jamaica (resembling gardens and bee-hives) with the same purpose and design they proposed to themselves in the Isle of Hispaniola, perpetrating innumerable robberies and villanies as before; whereunto they added unheard of cruelties by murdering, burning, roasting, and exposing men to be torn to pieces by dogs; and finally by afflicting and harassing them with un-exampled oppressions and torments in the mines, they spoiled and unpeopled this country of these innocents. These two isles containing six

[16] In 1495, Queen Isabella prevented Columbus from selling Indians as slaves. On 1501, she instructed Nicolás de Ovando that she wished the inhabitants to be well treated as subjects and vassals.

[17] The Isle of San Juan is Puerto Rico, which was known as *San Juan Bautista* at the time.

hundred thousand at least, though at this day there are scarce two hundred men to be found in either of them, the remainder perishing without the knowledge of Christian faith or sacrament. [18]

OF THE ISLE OF CUBA

 http://bit.ly/cub-brief

In the year of our Lord 1511, the Spanish[19] passed over to Cuba, which contains as much ground in length as there is distance between *Valladolid* and *Rome*, well furnished with large and stately provinces and very populous, against whom they proceeded with no more humanity and clemency, or indeed to speak truth with greater savageness and brutality. Several memorable transactions worthy observation, passed in this island. a certain Cacique a potent peer, named Hatuey, who not long before fled from Hispaniola to Cuba for refuge from death, or captivity during life; and understanding by certain Indians that the Spaniards intended to steer their course thither, made this oration to all his people assembled together.

"You are not ignorant that there is a rumor spread abroad among us of the Spaniards arrival, and are sensible by woeful experience how such and such (naming them) and Haití" (so they term Hispaniola in their own language) "with their Inhabitants have been treated by them, that they design to visit us with equal intentions of committing such acts as they have hitherto been guilty of. But do you not know the cause and reason of their coming? We are altogether ignorant of it," they replied, "but sufficiently satisfied that they are cruelly and wickedly inclined." Then thus, he said, "they adore a certain covetous deity, whose cravings are not to be satisfied by a few moderate offerings, but they may answer his adoration and worship, demand many unreasonable things of us, and use their utmost endeavors to subjugate and afterwards murder us." Then taking up a cask or cabinet near at hand,

---

[18] The expeditions of Juan Ponce de León and Juan de Esquivel to San Juan and Jamaica, respectively, are discussed in more detail in another book by Friar Bartolomé de las Casas, History of the Indies (book 2, chapters 46 – 55).

[19] The Cuba expedition was under the command of Diego Velázquez.

full of gold and gems, he proceeded in this manner: "This is the Spaniard's God, and in honor of him if you think well of it, let us celebrate our *areytos*" (which are certain kinds of dances used among them); "and by this means his deity being appeased, he will impose his commands on the Spaniards that they shall not for the future molest us; who all unanimously with one consent in a loud tone made this reply. Well said, well said," and thus they continued skipping and dancing before this cabinet, without the least intermission, till they were quite tired and grown weary. Then, the noble Hatuey re-assuming his discourse, said, "if we worship this deity, till ye be ravished from us, we shall be destroyed, therefore I judge it convenient, upon mature deliberation, that we cast it into the river," which advice was approved of by all without opposition, and the cabinet thrown in to the next river.

When the Spaniards first touched this Island, this Cacique, who was thoroughly acquainted with them, did avoid and shun them as much as in him lay, and defended himself by force of arms, wherever he met with them, but at length being taken he was burnt alive, for flying from so unjust and cruel a nation, and endeavoring to secure his life against them, who only thirsted after the blood of himself and his own people. Now being bound to the post, in order of his execution a certain holy monk of the Franciscan order, discoursed with him concerning God and the articles of our faith, which he never heard of before, and which might be satisfactory and advantageous to him, considering the small time allowed him by the executioner, promising him eternal glory and repose, if he truly believed them, or otherwise everlasting torments. After that Hatuey had been silently pensive sometime, he asked the monk whether the Spaniards also were admitted into heaven, and he answering that the gates of heaven were open to all that were good and godly, the Cacique replied without further consideration, that he would rather go to hell then heaven, for fear he should cohabit in the same mansion with so sanguinary and bloody a nation. And thus, God and the Holy Catholic Faith are praised and reverenced by the practices of the Spaniards in America.

Illustration 6: De Bry, Theodor, ca. 1598. Cacique prefers to go to hell rather than meet in heaven with Christians. [engraving]. On: Brevíssima relación de la destruyción de las Indias. Frankfurt, 1598. 3D image on **http://bit.ly/lascasas6***.*

Once it so happened, that the citizens of a famous city, distant ten leagues from the place where we then resided, came to meet us with a splendid retinue, to render their visit more honorable, bringing with them delicious viands, and such kind of dainties, with as great a quantity of fish as they could possibly procure, and distributing them among us; but behold on a sudden, some wicked devil possessing the minds of the Spaniards, agitated them with great fury, that I being present, and without the least pretense or occasion offered, they cut off in cold blood above three thousand men, women and children promiscuously, such inhumanities and barbarisms were committed in my sight, as no age can parallel.

Sometime after I dispatched messengers to all the rulers of the province of Havana (acting on assurances I obtained from our commander[20]), that they would by no means be terrified, or seek their refuge by absence and flight, but to meet us; and that I would engage (for they understood my authority) that they should not receive the least of injuries; for the whole country was extremely afflicted at the evils and mischiefs already perpetrated, and this I did with the advice of their captain. As soon as we approached the province, twenty one of their noblemen came forth to meet us, whom the captain contrary to his faith given, would have exposed to the flames, alleging that it was expedient they should be put to death, who were, at any time, capacitated to use any stratagem against us, but with great difficulty and much ado, I snatched them out of the fire.

These Islanders of Cuba, being reduced to the same vassalage and misery as the inhabitants of Hispaniola, seeing themselves perish and die without any redress, fled to the mountains for shelter, but others desperate, put a period to their days with a halter, and the husband, together with his wife and children, hanging himself, put an end to those calamities. By the ferocity of one Spanish tyrant (whom I knew) above two hundred Indians hanged themselves of their own accord; and a multitude of people perished by this kind of death.

---

[20] Pánfilo de Narváez. He had participated in the conquest of Cuba and led an army to Mexico in an unsuccessful attempt to wrest control of the country from Hernán Cortés. He captained an expedition to Florida in 1527. In 1528, he was the first European to land on the coast of what is today Venezuela.

A certain person here in the same isle constituted to exercise a kind of royal power, happened to have three hundred Indians fall to his share, of which in three months, through excessive labor, two hundred and seventy were destroyed, insomuch that in a short space there remained but a tenth part alive, namely thirty, but when the number was doubled, they all perished at the same rate, and all that were bestowed upon him lost their lives, till at length he paid his last debt to nature and the devil.

In three- or four-months' time I was there present, 7000 children and upward were murdered, because they had lost their parents who labored in the mines; nay I was a witness of many other stupendous villainies.

But afterward they consulted how to persecute those that lay hid in the mountains, who were miserably massacred, and consequently this Isle made desolate, which I saw not long after, and certainly it is a dreadful and deplorable sight to behold it thus unpeopled and laid waste, like a desert.

OF THE CONTINENT

http://bit.ly/tie-brief

In the year 1514, a certain unhappy governor[21] landed on the firm land or continent[22], a most bloody tyrant, destitute of all mercy and prudence, the instrument of God's wrath, with a resolution to people these parts with Spaniards; and although some tyrants had touched here before him, and cruelty hurried them into the other world by several ways of slaughter, yet they came no farther than to the sea coast, where they committed prodigious thefts and robberies, but this person exceeded all that ever dwelt in other islands, though execrable and profligate villains. For he did not only ravage and depopulate the seacoast but buried the largest regions and most ample kingdoms in their own ruins, sending thousands to hell by

---

[21] Pedro Árias deÁvila.

[22] Name given to northern South América and southern Central América.

his butcheries. He made incursions for many leagues continuance, that is to say, in those countries that are included in the territories of Darien and the provinces of Nicaragua, where are near five hundred leagues of the most fertile land in the world, and the most opulent for gold of all the regions hitherto discovered. And although Spain has been sufficiently furnished with the purest gold, yet it was diged out of the bowels and mines of the said countries by the Indians, where (as we have said) they perished.

This ruler, with his accomplices found out new inventions to rack, torment, force and extort gold from the Indians. One of his captains in a certain excursion undertaken by the command of his governor to make depredations, destroyed forty thousand persons and better exposing them to the edge of the sword, fire, dogs and variety of torments; of all which a religious man of the order of St. Francis, Franciscus de S. Romano, who was then present was an eye-witness.

Great and injurious was the pernicious blindness over the Indians; as to the conversion and salvation of this people: for they denied in effect what they in their flourishing discourse pretended to, and declared with their tongue what they contradicted in their heart; for it came to this pass, that the Indians should be commanded by on the penalty of a bloody war, death, and perpetual bondage, to embrace the Christian faith, and submit to the obedience of the Spanish King; as if the son of God, who suffered death for the redemption of all mankind, had enacted a law, when he pronounced these words, go and teach all nations that infidels, living peaceably and quietly in their hereditary native country, should be imposed upon pain of confiscation of all their chattels, lands, liberty, wives, children, and death itself, without any precedent instruction to confess and acknowledge the true God, and subject themselves to a King, whom they never saw, or heard mentioned before; and whose messengers behaved themselves toward them with such inhumanity and cruelty as they had done hitherto. Which is certainly a most foppish and absurd way of proceeding, and merits nothing but scandal, derision, nay hell itself. Now suppose this notorious and profligate governor had been empowered to see the execution of these edicts performed, for of themselves they were repugnant both to law and equity; yet he commanded (or they who were to see the execution thereof, did it of their own heads without authority) that when they fancied or proposed to themselves any place, that was well stored with gold, to rob and feloniously steal it away from the Indians living in their cities and houses, without the least suspicion of any ill act. These wicked Spaniards, like thieves came to any place by stealth, half a mile off of any city, town or village, and there in the night published and proclaimed the edict among themselves after this manner:

"You Caciques and Indians of this continent, the inhabitants of such a place, which they named; We declare or be it known to you all, that there is but one God, one hope, and one King of Castile, who is lord of these countries; appear forth without delay, and take the oath of allegiance to the Spanish King, as his vassals."

So about the fourth watch of the night, or three in the morning these poor innocents overwhelmed with heavy sleep, ran violently on that place they named, set fire to their hovels[23], which were all thatch, and so, without notice, burnt men, women and children; killed whom they pleased upon the spot; but those they preserved as captives, were compelled through torments to confess where they had hid the gold, when they found little or none at their houses; but they who lived being first stigmatized, were made slaves; yet after the fire was extinguished, they came hastily in quest of the gold.

Thus did this wicked man, devoted to all the infernal furies, behave himself with the assistance of profligate Christians, whom he had lifted in his service from the 14th to the 21th or 22nd year, together with his domestic servants and followers, from whom he received as many portions, besides what he had from his slaves in gold, pearls, and jewels, as the chief governor would have taken, and all that were constituted to execute any kind of kingly office followed in the same footsteps; every one sending as many of his servants as he could spare, to share in the spoil. Nay he that came hither and the Bishop[24] first of all did the same also, and at the very time (as I conjecture) the Spaniards did depredate or rob this kingdom of above one million castilians[25] of gold: Yet all these their thefts and felonies, we scarce find upon record that three thousand castilians ever came into the Spanish King's coffers; yet there were above eight hundred thousand men slain: The

---

[23] Hut.

[24] Friar Juan Quevedo.

[25] The castilian was a 1.6 oz gold coin worth 480 *maravedies*.

other tyrants who governed this kingdom afterward to the three and thirtieth year, deprived all of them of life that remained among the inhabitants.

Among all those flagitious acts committed by this governor while he ruled this kingdom, or by his consent and permission this must by no means be omitted: A certain Cacique, bestowing on him a gift, voluntarily, or (which is more probably) induced thereunto by fear, about the weight of nine thousand castelians, but the Spaniards not satisfied with so fast a sum of money, seize him, fix him to a pole; extended his feet, which being moved near the fire, they demanded a larger sum; the Cacique overcome with torments, sending home, procured three thousand more to be brought and presented to them: But the Spaniards, adding new torments to new rage and fury, when they found he would confer no more upon them, which was because he could not, or otherwise because he would not, they exposed him for so long to that torture, till by degrees of heat the marrow gushed out of the soles of his feet, and so he died; Thus they often murdered the lords and nobles which such torments to extort the gold from them.

One time it happened that a century or party of one hundred Spaniards making excursions, came to a mountain, where many people shunning so horrid and pernicious an enemy concealed themselves, who immediately rushing on them, putting all to the sword they could meet with, and then secured seventy or eighty married women as well as virgins captives; but a great number of Indians with a fervent desire of recovering their wives and daughters appeared in arms against the Spaniards, and when they drew near the enemy, they unwilling to lose the prey, run the wives and maidens through with their swords. The Indians through grief and trouble, smiting their breasts, brake out into these exclamations. "O perverse generation of men! O cruel Spaniards! What did you murder las Iras?" (In their language they call women by the name of *las iras* as if they had said: "to slay women is an act of bloody-minded men, worse than brutes and wild beasts."

There was the house of a puissant[26] potentate situated about ten or fifteen leagues from Panamá, whose name was Paris, very rich in gold; and the Spaniards gave him a visit, who were entertained with fraternal kindness, and courteously received, and of his own accord, presented the captain with

---

[26] Mighty, powerful.

a gift of fifteen thousand castelians; who was of opinion, as well as the rest of the Spaniards, that he who bestowed such a quantity of money gratis, was the master of vast treasure; whereupon they counterfeit a pretended departure, but returning about the fourth night-watch, and entering the city privily upon a surprise, which they thought was sufficiently secured, consecrated it with many citizens to the flames, and robbed them of fifty or sixty thousand castelians. the dynast or Prince escaped with his life, and gathering together as great a number of men as he could possibly at that instant of time, and three or four days being elapsed, pursued the Spaniards, who had deprived him also by violence and rapine of a hundred and thirty or forty thousand castelians, and pouring in upon them, recovered all his gold with the destruction of fifty Spaniards. But the remainder of them having received many wounds in that reencounter betook them to their heels and saved themselves by flight. A few days after the Spaniards return, and fall upon the said Cacique well-armed and overthrow him and all his forces, and they who out-lived the combat, to their great misfortune, were exposed to the usual and frequently mentioned bondage.

OF THE PROVINCE OF NICARAGUA

http://bit.ly/nic-brief

The said tyrant[27] Ann. Dom. 1522. proceeded farther very unfortunately to the subjugation of conquest of this province. In truth no person can satisfactorily or sufficiently express the fertility, temperateness of the climate, or the multitude of the inhabitants of Nicaragua, which was almost infinite and admirable; for this region contained some cities that were four leagues long; and the abundance of fruits of the earth (which was the cause of such a concourse of people) was highly commendable. The people of this place, because the country was level and plain, destitute of mountains, so very delightful and pleasant, that they could not leave it without great grief, and much dissatisfaction. They were therefore tormented with the greater vexations and persecutions, and forced to bear

---

[27] Pedrarias Dávila.

the Spanish tyranny and servitude, which as much patience as they were masters of: Add further that they were peaceable and meek spirited. This tyrant with these accomplices of his cruelty did afflict this nation (whose advice he made use of in destroying the other kingdoms) with such and so many great damages, slaughters, injustice, slaver, and barbarisms, that a tongue, though of iron, could not express them all fully. He sent into the province (which is larger than the county of Ruscínia) fifty horse-men, who put all the people to the edge of the sword, sparing neither age nor sex upon the most trivial and inconsiderable occasion: As for example, if they did not come to them with all possible speed, when called; and bring the imposed burthen of *mahid* (which signifies corn in their dialect) or if they did not bring the number of Indians required to his own, and the service or rather servitude of his associates. And the country being all campaign or level, no person was able to withstand the hellish fury of their horses.

He commanded the Spaniards to make excursions, that is, to rob other provinces, permitting and granting these thieving rogues leave to take away by force as many of these peaceable people as they could, who being ironed[28] (that they might not sink under the burthen of sixty or eighty pound weight) it frequently happened, that of four thousand Indians, six only returned home, and so they died by road. But, if any of them chanced to faint, being tired with over-weighty burthens, or through great hunger and thirst should be seized with a distemper; or too much debility and weakness, that they might not spend time in taking off their fetters, they beheaded them, so the head fell one way, and the body another: The Indians when they spied the Spaniards making preparations for such journeys, knowing very well, that few, or none returned home alive, just upon their setting out with sighs and tears, burst out into these or the like expressions: "Those were journeys, which we travelled frequently in the service of Christians, and in some tract of time we returned to our habitations, wives and children: But now there being no hope of a return, we are forever deprived of their family's sight and conversation."

It happened also, that the same president would dissipate or disperse the Indians *de novo* at his own pleasure, to force the Indians away from those (conquerors) he didn't like; and dispose of them to others; upon which it

---

[28] Tied with iron chains.

fell out, that for the space of a year complete, there was no sowing or planting; And when they wanted bread, the Spaniards took it from the Indians by force, thus plunder the Indians of the whole stock of corn that they had laid up for the support of their families, and by these indirect courses above twenty or thirty thousand perished with hunger. Nay it fortuned at one time, that a woman oppressed with insufferable hunger, deprived her own son of his life to preserve her own.

In this Province also they brought many to an untimely end, loading their shoulders with heavy planks and pieces of timber, which they were compelled to carry to a harbor forty leagues distant, to build ships. Likewise, they sent them to the mountains to find honey and wax, where they were devoured by tigers; and pregnant women and with newborns carrying burdens as if they were beasts.

But no greater pest was there that could unpeople this Province, than the license granted to Spaniards by this governor, to demand captives from Caciques and potentates of this region. Each other four or five months, or as often as they obtained the grace of the governor to demand them, they delivered them fifty servants, and the Spaniards terrified them with menaces, that if they did not obey them in answering their unreasonable demands, they should be burnt alive, or baited to death by dogs. Now the Indians are but slenderly stored with servants; for it is much if a Cacique had three or four in his retinue[29]. Therefore, they have resorted to their subjects; and after they had, in the first place, seized the orphans, they required earnestly and instantly one son of the parent, who had but two, and two of him that had but three, and for the lord of the place satisfied the desires of the tyrant, not without the effusion of tears and groans of the people, who (as it seems) were very careful of their children. And this being frequently repeated in the space between the year 1523, and 1533, the kingdom lost all their inhabitants, for in six or seven years' time there were constantly five or six ships made ready to be freighted with Indians that were sold in the regions of Panamá and *Perú*, where they all died; for it is by daily experience proved and known, that the Indians when transported out of their native country into any other, soon die; because they are shortened in their allowance of food, and the task imposed on them no ways diminished, them being only bought for labor.

---

[29] Court.

And by this means, there have been taken out of this province five hundred thousand inhabitants and upward, who were before freemen, and made slaves. "In this way, more than five hundred thousand Indian souls from this province, being as free[30] as I am, have been made slaves.

Because of the wars made on them, and the horrid bondage they were reduced unto, more than fifty or sixty hundred have perished, and to this day very many still are destroyed. Now all these Slaughters have been committed within the space of fourteen years inclusively. Possibly, in this province of Nicaragua there remains four or five thousand men who are put to death by ordinary and personal oppressions, whereas (according to what is said already) it did exceed other countries of the world in multitude of people.

OF NEW SPAIN – PART ONE

http://bit.ly/nue-brief

New *Spain* was discovered Ann. Dom. 1517, and in the detection there was no first or second attempt, but all were exposed to slaughter. The year ensuing those Spaniards (who style themselves Christians) came thither to rob, kill and slay, though they pretend they undertook this voyage to people[31] the country. From year 1518 to the present, *viz.* 1542, the injustice, violence and tyranny of the Spaniards came to the highest degree of extremity: for they had shook hands with and bid adieu to all fear of God and the King, unmindful of themselves in this sad and deplorable condition. The destructions, cruelties, butcheries, devastations, the demolishing of cities, depredations, *&c.* which they perpetrated in so many and such ample kingdoms, are such and so great, and strike the minds of men with so great horror, that all we have related before are inconsiderable comparatively to those which have been acted from the year 1518 to 1542. To this very month of September that we now live to see the most heavy, grievous and detestable things are committed, that the rule

---

[30] Legally, all Indians were subjects of the Crown of Castill

[31] Populate.

we laid down before as a maxim might be indisputably verified, to wit, that from the beginning they ran headlong from bad to worse, and were overcome in their diabolical acts and wickedness only by themselves.

Thus from the first entrance of the Spaniards[32] into New Spain, which happened on the 18th day of April in the said month of the year 1518, to 1530 (the space of twelve whole years), there was no end or period put to the destruction and slaughters committed by the merciless hands of the sanguinary and blood-thirsty Spaniard in the continent, or space of 450 leagues round about Mexico, and the adjacent or neighboring parts, which might contain four or five spacious kingdoms, that neither for magnitude or fertility would give Spain herself the pre-eminence. This entire region was more populous than Toledo, Sevilla, Valladolid, Zaragoza, and Barcelona; and there is not at this day in all of them so many people, nor when they flourished in their greatest height and splendor was there such a number, as inhabited that region, which embraced in its circumference, four hundred and eighty leagues. Within these twelve years the Spaniards have destroyed in the said continent, by spears, fire and sword, including men, women, youth, and children above four million people in these their acquits or conquests (for under that word they mask their cruel actions) or rather those of the Turk himself, which are reported of them, tending to the ruin of the Catholic cause, together with their invasions and unjust wars, contrary to and condemned by divine as well as human laws. This is without counting the number who perished by their more tyrannical servitude, vexations and daily oppressions.

There is no tongue[33], art, or human knowledge can recite the horrid impieties, which these capital enemies to government and all mankind have been guilty of at several times and in several nations; nor can the circumstantial aggravations of some of their wicked acts be unfolded or displayed by any manner of industry, time or writing, but yet I will say somewhat of every individual particular thing, which this protestation and

---

[32] There were two trading expeditions led by Francisco Hernández de Córdoba (1517), and Juan de Grijalva (1518), without a formal intention to settle. The first fully equipped military expedition was led by Hernán Cortés, which left Cuba on 1519.

[33] Language.

oath, that I conceive I am not able to comprehend one of a thousand.

OF NEW SPAIN – PART TWO

http://bit.ly/nue2-brief

One of the slaughters they perpetrated was in the most spacious city of Cholula[34], which consisted of thirty thousand families. All the chief rulers of that region and neighboring places, starting with the priests and their Highest Priest meet the Spaniards in pomp and state. The Indians gave Spaniards a more reverential and honorable reception leading them to settle in the city, and to entertain in the apartments of the most powerful and principal noblemen. The Spaniards agreed to slaughter or castigate (as they term it) Indians right there to instill fear and bravery in every corner of this region for in all the countries that they came they took this course. Once they arrived, they committed notorious butcheries, which made those innocent sheep tremble for fear. For this purpose, they called the governors and nobles of the cities, and all places subject unto them, together with their supreme Lord, told they should appear before them, and no sooner did they attend in expectation of some capitulation or discourse with the Spanish commander, but they were presently seized upon and detained prisoners before anyone could advertise or give them notice of their captivity. They demanded of them five or six thousand Indians to carry their baggage; and as soon as they came the Spaniards locked in backyards. It was a pity to see these Indians when they appeared to carry the load because they were naked. Their bodies were only covered with a net over their shoulders containing their food. They were all in a squatting position, as meek lambs, all together in the courtyard. Then, the Spanish guards (who were armed) entered into the backyard and, with swords and spears did not spare one

---

[34] This was Cortés' most widely reported massacre. Cholula was the cult-centre of Quetzacoátl, the Mexican deity with whom Cortés is supposed to have been confused. Cortés reported 3000 dead, but another witness claimed the death toll was ten times higher.

sheep. No Indian was able to escape without being chopped.

But, after two or three days, some of Indians, who hid among the dead bodies, covered with blood, presented themselves to the Spaniards, imploring their mercy and the prolongation of their lives with tears in their eyes and all imaginable submission Yet the Spaniards, not in the least moved with pity or compassion, tore them up into pieces. In the case of chief governors, who were above one hundred in number, the Captain ordered to bound and affix them to posts, then burn them alive.

Illustration 7: De Bry, Theodor, ca. 1598. The determination was to make a killing so that the Indians would tremble like meek sheep [engraving]. On: Brevíssima relación de la destruyción de las Indias. Frankfurt, 1598. 3D image on **http://bit.ly/lascasas07.**

Yet, a lord that seemed to be the King of the land escaped and gathered twenty or thirty or forty men into a temple (called in their tongue *quu*), which he used as a castle or place of defense. But the Spaniards set fire to the temple, burnt all those that were inside, who were crying out these words: "Oh profligate men, what injury have we done you to occasion our death"

Go, go to Mexico, where our supreme Lord Moctezuma will revenge our cause upon your persons." And 'tis reported, while the Spaniards were engaged in this tragedy destroying six or seven thousand men, their commander with great rejoicing sang this arie:

"Mira Nero de Tarpeia,
Roma como se ardía.
Gritos de niños y viejot,
y él de nada se dolía."[35]

"From the Tarpeian,
still Nero espies
Rome all in flames with unrelenting eyes,
and hears of young an old the dreadful cries."

They committed another great butchery in Tepeara, a city that was larger and had more residents than the former; and here they massacred with swords with such much cruelty. an incredible number of Indians.

Setting sail from Cholula, they steered their course to Mexico[36], where King Montezuma sent his nobles and peers with abundance of presents to greet them. The King's brother brought gold, silver, and clothes as presents. When the retinue got closer to the city gates, the King himself appeared carried in a golden litter, with the whole court, and attended them to the palace that was prepared for their reception.

Some of the people who were present told that King Moctezuma was made a prisoner[37] and put into the custody of eighty guards, who chained him. Many things can be said about the things they did that day, but I will just tell about this one that may merit your observation. The Spanish Captain left to take prisoner another so called Captain[38] that was against him. He left

---

[35] A traditional Spanish ballad.

[36] Las Casas means Tenochtitlán, capital of the Aztec empire.

[37] According to Cortés, Moctezuma was seized more than a week later.

[38] The first Captain was Hernán Cortés, and the other was Pánfilo de Narváez.

Moctezuma with about one hundred men to guard him. Those men[39] agreed to act something worth remembrance, to make Indians even more scared.

*Illustration 8: De Bry, Theodor, ca. 1598. They took Moctezuma captive the same day he brought presents for the Spanish [engraving]. On: Brevissima relación de la destruyción de las Indias. Frankfurt, 1598. 3D image on **http://bit.ly/lascasas08**.*

In the meantime, all the nobility and commonality of the city thought of nothing else, but how to exhilarate the spirit of their captive king, and solace him during his confinement with a variety of diversions and recreations.

Among the festivities they conducted were afternoon dances across neighborhoods and public squares they called *mirotes* (a concept similar to the *areytos* that were celebrated on the Islands). They drew all their finery and riches, and this was part of their way of rejoicing. The noblest and knights and of royal blood, according to their grades, did their dancing for the houses closest to where their King was imprisoned. In the part closest to the palaces

---

[39] Led by Pedro de Alvarado, second in-command-to Cortés.

there were over 2,000 sons of lords, which was all the flower and cream of the nobility of the entire Montezuma empire. Towards these the captain of the Spaniards went, and sent other crews the other parts of the city where the parties were being celebrated. Concealing how they were going to see them they agreed to ram the Indians at a certain time.

When the Indians were concentrated in their activities, the Captain said, "Santiago[40] and them," and Spaniards began, with their bare swords, to cut those naked and delicate bodies to shed generous blood. They left no one alive, did the same in the other squares. It was a thing that left Indians in mourning, stunned, distraught, and swollen with bitterness and pain. From here to the end of the world, or that they ended, they will not stop regretting and singing in their *areytos* and dances as in romances (as in Spain we say) that calamity and loss of the succession of all their nobility, that they prized so many years ago.

---

[40] Santiago is the name of St. James of Compostela, and his name was used as a battle-cry, according to a legend that he appeared in person, mounted on a white horse at the Battle of Clavijo against the Moors, which took place in year 822.

Illustration 9: De Bry, Theodor, ca. 1598. Loss of succession of all nobility [engraving]. On: Brevíssima relación de la destruyción de las Indias. Frankfurt, 1598. 3D image on **http://bit.ly/lascasas09.**

Having never seen the Indians something so unfair and cruel done to so many innocent people without guilt, and after having tolerated the unjust imprisonment of their King (because he himself commanded them not to rush or war the Christians), then the Indians raised weapons through the city. They hurt a lot of Spaniards that they could barely escape. Then they put a dagger in the chest to the prisoner Moctezuma to order the Indians to stop fighting and be at peace. The Indians did not obey him at all, preferring to talk about the election of another King and captain to guide their battles. The Captain who had gone to fight at the port was already coming back victorious and accompanied by more Christians. The Indians continued fighting for three or four more days until the Captain entered the city. Then, they obtained assistance from an infinite number of people who came to the city and fought in such a way and for so many days that, fearing all to die, the Spaniards agreed one night to leave the city. When the Indians learned of the departure, they killed a large number of Christians on the bridges of the lagoon. This was a holy war, for just causes that anyone who was reasonable and just would justify them. After the battle of the city, the Christians reformed, they wreaked havoc on the Indians who were admirable and strange, they killed infinite people and burned many and great lords.

After the great and abominable tyrannies that they made in Mexico City and along about 10, 15, or 20 leagues from Mexico, (where an infinite number of people died), the Spaniards continued with their tyrannical pestilence and went to ravage the province of Pánuco, which was an admirable thing the multitude of the people that were there and the ravages and massacres that the Spaniards did.

Then, they similarly destroyed the provinces of Tututepeque, Ipilcingo, and Colima, which each had more land than the kingdom of León and that of Castile. Telling the ravages and deaths and cruelties they did in each one would undoubtedly be a very difficult and impossible thing to say and to listen to.

It is here to notice that the mandate with which they arrived and the reason why they destroyed all those innocent people and depopulated those lands (which so much joy they should cause to those who were true Christians with their large and infinite population) was to say that they should submit and obey the King of Spain. They were to kill and make slaves. If the Indians did not fulfill such irrational and foolish requests and put themselves in the hands of such wicked and cruel and bestial men, they would be called rebels and raised against the service of His Majesty, so they wrote here to the King our lord.

And the blindness of those who ruled the Indies did not reach or understand what in its laws is express and clearer than another of its principles, it is convenient to know: that neither is nor can be called a rebel if he is not a subject first. Consider Christians who know about God and reason, and even about human laws, could the hearts of people who live safely on their lands and don't know that they owe anything to anyone, and who have their natural lords, be stopped when a stranger comes to tell them: "Give yourselves to obey a strange King that you never saw or heard, and if not, we will tear them apart," especially seeing from experience that they do so later. And what is most frightening is that, to those who in fact obey, they are put in the utmost serfdom, where with incredible works and torments that last longer than if they were killed with the sword. In the end they and their wives, children and all their generation perished.

The tyrant Captain sent two more crueler, fierce, worse, and less merciful and merciful Captains than he, to two great, blooming, happy kingdoms that were full and populated with people. These were the kingdom of Guatemala, which is to the South Sea, and the other from Naco, Honduras or Guaimura, which is to the North Sea. They are border places and were three hundred leagues from Mexico. One of the captains went by land and the other on ships by sea, each with many people on horseback and standing. What they both did was so bad (especially the one that went to Guatemala[41], because the other[42] one had a bad death), that I could collect so many stories of evils, ravages, deaths, depopulations, so many and so fierce injustices that frightened the present centuries and to come and make them an extensive book, because it exceeded all past and present, both in the amount and number of abominations, as of the people it destroyed and lands it made deserted.

The one who went by sea in ships made great robberies and scandals in the coastal towns, when they were received with presents in the kingdom of Yucatan (which is on the road to the kingdoms of Naco or Guaimura, where it was going). After he arrived, he sent Captains and many people all over that land, where they robbed, killed, and destroyed towns and people. One of the Captains rose with three hundred men and went inside to Guatemala, destroying and burning how many villages he found, and robbing and killing his residents. And he was doing this for more than one hundred and twenty leagues. When someone was sent after him, they found the land unpopulated, the Indians raised and willing to kill in revenge for the damage and destruction they left behind.

A few days after they killed the main captain who sent them, to whom he rose, then many other very tyrant tyrants followed that with slaughter, frightful cruelty, and making the Indian slaves and selling them to the ships

---

[41] Pedro de Alvarado.

[42] Cristóbal de Olid.

that brought wine, dresses, and others. stuff.

With the tyrannical ordinary servitude, from the year of one thousand five hundred and twenty-four to the year of one thousand and five hundred and thirty-five, those provinces and kingdom of Naco or Honduras ravaged, which truly looked like a paradise of delights and were more populated than the most frequented and populated land that can be in the world.

Now that we passed and came through them, we saw them so depopulated and destroyed that anyone, no matter how hard it was, would open their guts of pain. In these eleven years more than two stories of souls have died, and about two thousand people have remained in a block of more than 100 leagues. Those who remain are dying in servitude.

But to return to that great Tyrant, who outdid the former in cruelty (as hinted above) and is equal to those that tyrannize there at present, who travelled to Guatemala. He did make it to his urgent and daily business to procure ruin and destruction by slaughter, fire, and depopulations, compelling all to submit to the Spanish King, whom Indians looked upon to be more unjust and crueler than his inhumane and bloodthirsty ministers.

OF THE PROVINCE OF GUATEMALA

 http://bit.ly/gua-brief

U pon reaching the kingdom, there was a lot of killing of people. This, despite the fact that the main lord and others from the city of Utatlán came out to receive him in walks and with trumpets, *atabales* and many parties, giving the Spaniards to eat and the more they could. That night the Spaniards settled outside the city, because they understood that the kingdom was strong and that they would be in danger inside. On another day they called the main lord and many others. When they arrived like meek sheep, they were arrested and asked to be given so many loads of gold. The lords replied that they did not have, because that land was not golden. Then they were sent to burn alive, with no other fault, no other process or sentence. Since they saw the lords of all the provinces that had burned that man and his supreme companions only because they did not give them gold, they fled all of their villages getting into the mountains, and sent all their people to go to the Spanish and serve as gentlemen, but do not tell them where they were hiding. All the people of the land came to tell the Spaniards that they wanted to be theirs and serve them as lords. The pious captain said he did not want to receive them, and that they would kill them if they did not discover where their lords were. The Indians answered that they did not know about their lords. That they could go find them themselves and, in their homes, they would find them. There they could kill them or make them whatever they wanted. This is what the Indians said and did many times. And it was wonderful: that the Spaniards went to the villages where the poor people were working in their offices, with their wives and children safe. There they speared them, and the great and powerful people came and almost ravaged them in a matter of two hours, nailing the sword to children, women and old people.

Once the Indians noticed that with such humility, offers, patience and suffering they could not break or soften such inhuman and beastly hearts, and that without appearance or color of reason they broke them apart, noting that they died just as well, they agreed to convene and gather all and die in the war, taking revenge as they could of such cruel and infernal enemies.

Knowing that they could not prevail being unarmed, naked, on foot, and skinny, fighting against fierce people on horseback, and so well armed, they invented some holes in the middle of the roads where the horses would fall and the Spanish would gut with stakes that would be placed inside the holes. The traps would be covered with herbs that seemed to have nothing. Only one or two horses fell, because the Spaniards knew how to take care of themselves, but in order to take revenge, the Spaniards made a law that all Indians of all genders and ages were thrown into the holes, and thus pregnant and birthing women, children, and old men threw themselves in the holes until they were pierced by the stakes. It was a shame to see, especially women with their children.

Everyone else was shot and slashed. They threw the brave dogs that ripped them apart and ate; and when some man ran into it, they honorably burned it in living flames. They were in these butcher shops so inhuman for about seven years, from the year of twenty-four to the year of thirty or thirty-one. You will be able to judge here how many people perished.

Illustration 10: De Bry, Theodor, ca. 1598. Women, children and old people were thrown into holes where they would be pierced by stakes [engraving]. On: Brevíssima relación de la destruyción de las Indias. Frankfurt, 1598. 3D image on **http://bit.ly/lascasa10**.

This poorly risky tyrant and his brothers did infinite horrible works in this kingdom (because they were his captains, no less unhappy and insensitive than he). They went to the province of Cuzcatán, where or near where the town of San Salvador is located, which is a very happy land, with the entire southern seacoast measuring between forty and fifty leagues.

In the city of Cuzcatán, which was the head of the province, they made a great reception. Between twenty and thirty thousand Indians were waiting for him loaded with chickens and food. Having arrived and received the present, the tyrant ordered each Spaniard to take all the Indians they wanted so that they would use them the days they were there. Each one took a hundred or fifty, or those that seemed to be enough. The innocent lambs served with all their strength, which was not lacking but to worship them. In the meantime, this captain asked the principals to bring him a lot of gold, because they mainly came to that. The Indians responded that they were happy to give them all the gold they had, and a large number of golden

45

copper axes that look like gold, because they had some. The Captain sent for a test, and since he saw that it was copper, he told the Spaniards: «Give this land to hell. Let us go, because there is no gold, and each one throw chains to the Indians they have, which I will send to mark as slaves. They did so and they were blackened with the King's mark, and I saw the wounded forehead of the chief lord of that city. The escaped Indians saw this and joined with others from the surrounding lands to fight with weapons.

The Spaniards made great ravages and killings with them. They founded Guatemala, where they built a city, which was prosecuted with three floods together: one of water, another of land and another of stones as thick as between ten and twenty oxen. Having died all the lords and men who could make war, the Spaniards put those who remained in the abovementioned infernal servitude. They sent ships loaded with them to sell to Peru, and with other massacres and ravages, they have destroyed and ravaged a kingdom of more than one hundred leagues in block, of the happiest in fertility and population that could be in the world. And this tyrant himself wrote that it was more populated than the kingdom of Mexico, and he said the truth: more has he and his brothers[43] died with the others between four and five million souls in fifteen or sixteen years, from the year of 1524 to 1540. Today, they kill and destroy those that remain, and they will do so with others.

He had this custom: that when he was going to make war on some towns or provinces he carried as many as he could of the enslaved Indians. Since he did not feed between ten and twenty thousand men he wore, he allowed them to eat the Indians. And so, there was in his real solemn carnage of human flesh, where in his presence children were killed and roasted, and men were killed only by the hands and feet, which they had for the best bites. And with these inhumanities, hearing them the other people of the other lands, they did not know where to hide from horror.

[43] Gonzalo, Gómez and Jorge de Alvarado.

Illustration 11: De Bry, Theodor, ca. 1598. Human butchers taking the meat of the Indians to feed the Spanish troops [engraving]. On: Brevíssima relación de la destruyción de las Indias. Frankfurt, 1598. 3D imagen on **http://bit.ly/lascasas11.**

He killed infinite people in the construction of ships. Towards that the Indians loaded anchors that weighed between three and four *quintales*[44] by an extension of 130 leagues, from north to south. Thus, the sad naked ones carried much artillery on their shoulders, and I saw many distressed by the burden on the roads. The Captain took the women and daughters of the Indians to give them to the sailors and soldiers, thus having them happy to carry them in their navies. They filled the ships with Indians, where everyone died of thirst and hunger. If I were to say their cruelties in particular, I would make a great book that would frighten the world. He made two navies of many ships each, with which he burned all those lands as if the sky were fire. Oh how many orphans he made, how many he stole from his children, how many he deprived of his women, how many women he left without husbands, how many adulteries and stupid and violent acts he caused, how many deprived of his freedom, how many anguish and calamities many

---

[44] Each *quintal* weighs 100 pounds.

people suffered for him, how many tears did she shed, how many sighs, how many groans, how many loneliness in this life, and how much eternal damnation he caused: not only from Indians, who were infinite, but from the unhappy Christians whose consortium favored in grave sins and abominations. And pray to God that from him there has been mercy and be content with as bad an end as it happened.

OF NEW SPAIN, PANUCO AND XALISCO

http://bit.ly/pan-brief

After the great cruelties and massacres said and those that I have stopped saying about the provinces of New Spain, another cruel callous tyrant[45] was in the Pánuco year 1525. Making many cruelties and marking a large number of slaves, which were all free men, and sending many loaded ships to the islands of Cuba and Spain to sell them, finished ravaging the entire province and there was an exchange of eighty Indians, rational souls, for a mare.

The Captain was assigned the mission of governing Mexico City and all of New Spain, accompanied by other tyrants with the role of judges and he as president. Among them, they committed such great evils, sins, cruelties, robberies and abominations that they have left all that land in such depopulation that if God did not attack them with the resistance of the religious of St. Francis and then with the provision of a Royal Audience[46] (good and friend of all virtue), in two years they will leave New Spain as is currently Hispaniola island.

There was a man of those who, to enclose a large garden, had eight thousand Indians working without paying them anything or feeding them.

---

[45] Beltrán Nuño de Guzmán.

[46] The Audiencias of Chanceries were courts of justice presided by a high-ranking churchman but staffed by lawyers. Audiencias in the Indies had more authority over government than their counterparts in Spain.

They died of hunger, and he didn't even take it for granted. Since the main news (the one I said that had just ravaged Pánuco) that the Royal Hearing was coming, he invented to go inland and forcibly took fifteen or twenty thousand men out of the province of Mexico to carry the charges. Of these, only about 200 returned alive. He arrived in the province of Mechuacán, which is forty leagues from Mexico, and the King and lord of the place received him with a procession of infinite people and giving him a thousand services and gifts. The Spaniards captured the said King because he was reputed to be rich and have a lot of gold and silver. The tyrant began to torture him. They put him in stocks by the feet, the body extended and tied by the hands to a tree and put a brazier next to the feet. A boy with a swab dipped in oil sprayed them occasionally to toast well. On one side of the Lord was a Christian with an armed crossbow pointed at his heart. On the other side, another man was throwing him a terrible brave dog, which in a creed would tear him apart. And so, they tormented him to discover the treasures he had, until a certain St. Francis religious took it out of his hands, of which torments finally died. And in this way, they tormented and killed many lords and chieftains in those provinces to give them gold and silver.

Illustration 12: De Bry, Theodor, ca. 1598. Torture of the King of the province of Mechoacán to discover its treasures [engraving]. On: Brevíssima relación de la destruyción de las Indias. Frankfurt, 1598. 3D image on **http://bit.ly/casas12.**

A certain tyrant at that time, he was a *visitor* to the Indians (more aware of the bags and farms, than of the souls or people) to rob them. He found that certain Indians had their idols hidden. As if the sad Spanish had never been taught another better God, he arrested the Indians until they gave him idols, believing they were made of gold or silver, for which he cruelly and unjustly punished them. And because he was disappointed in his purpose, which was to steal, he forced the said chiefs to buy his idols, and bought them for the gold or silver they could find, to worship them, as they used to, for God's sake! These are the works and examples they do and honor that the unfortunate Spaniards seek to God in the Indies.

This great tyrant captain went from the province of Mechuacán to Jalisco, which was whole and full like a hive of people, very populated and very happy, because it is one of the most fertile and admirable in the Indies. The population extended by almost seven leagues. When they entered it, the lords and people received them with a gift and joy, as all Indians usually receive people. He began to do the cruelties and evils that used to be, and that everyone there has a habit, and many more, to achieve the end they have, for God's sake, which is gold. He burned the villages, seized the chiefs, gave them torments, enslaved the Indians and carried infinites tied in chains. Newly born women, carrying the burdens of bad Christians, could not take creatures for work. Because of the hunger weakness, they were thrown down the roads, where infinites perished. An evil Christian, forcibly taking a maiden to sin with her, attacked the mother to take her away. He drew a dagger or sword to cut off a hand to the mother, and the maid was stabbed to death because she did not correspond to the Christian's intention.

Illustration 13: De Bry, Theodor, ca. 1598. The women born were thrown down the road [engraving]. On: Brevíssima relación de la destruyción de las Indias. Frankfurt, 1598. 3D image on **http://bit.ly/lascasas13**.

The tyrant turned 4,500 Indians into slaves, including men, women, one-year-old children to the mothers' tits, and two, three, four, and five years, even when they came out to receive them peacefully, without other infinities that were not counted.

Finished the infinite wicked and infernal wars, and the killings he made in them, he put all that land in the ordinary and pestilential tyrannical servitude, which all the Christian tyrants of the Indies usually and pretend to put to those people. He consented that his own butlers and all others made cruelty and torments never heard of removing gold and tribute from the Indians.

The tyrant's butler killed many Indians by hanging them, burning them alive, throwing them to brave dogs, cutting off their feet, hands, heads and tongues, the Indians being of peace, with no other cause than to intimidate them, to serve him and give him gold and tributes. The tyrant egregious, seeing and knowing it, that many cruel scourges, sticks, slaps and other species of cruelty that they did to the Indians every day and every hour. In this Kingdom of Xalisco (according to report) they burnt eight hundred towns to ashes, and for this reason the Indians growing desperate, beholding the daily destruction of the remainders of their matchless cruelty, made an insurrection against the Spaniards, slew several of them justly and deservedly, and afterward fled to the insensible rocks and mountains (yet more tender and kind than the stony-hearted enemy) for sanctuary; where they were miserably massacred by those tyrants who succeeded, and there are now few, or none of the inhabitants to be found.

Thus the Spaniards being blinded with the luster of their gold, deserted by god, and given over to a reprobate sense, not understanding (or at least not willing to do so) that the cause of the Indians is most just, as well by the law of nature, as the divine and humane, they by force of arms, destroying them, hacking them in pieces, and turning them out of their own confines and dominions, nor considering how unjust that violence and tyrannies are, wherewith they have afflicted these poor creatures, they still contrive to raise new wars against them. Nay they conceive, and by word and writing testified, that those victories they have obtained against those innocents to their ruine, are granted them by God himself, as if their unjust wars were promoted and managed by a just right and title to what they pretend; and with boasting joy return thanks to God for their tyranny, in imitation of those tyrants and robbers, of whom the Prophet Zechariah part of the fourth and fifth verses. "Feed the sheep of the slaughter, whose possessors slay them, and hold themselves not guilty, and they that sell them say, blessed by the Lord, for ye are rich."

OF THE KINGDOM OF YUCATÁN

http://bit.ly/yuc-brief

An impious wretch, by his fabulous stories and relations to the King of Spain, was made prefect of the kingdom of Yucatan, in the year of our Lord 1526. Other tyrants[47] to this very day have taken the same indirect measures to obtain offices, and screw or wheedle themselves into public charges or employments, for this pretext, and authority, they had the greater opportunity to commit theft and rapine. This kingdom was very well peopled, and both for temperature of air, and the plenty of food and fruits, in which respect it is more fertile than *Mexico*, but chiefly for honey and wax, it exceeds all the Indian countries that had hitherto been discovered. It is three hundred leagues in compass. The inhabitants of this place excel all other Indians, either in polite or prudence, or in leading a regular life and morality, truly deserving to be instructed in the knowledge of the true God. Here the Spaniards might have erected many fair cities and lived as it were in a garden of delights, if they had not, through covetousness, stupidity, and the weight of enormous crimes rendered themselves unworthy of so great a benefit.

This tyrant, with three hundred men began to make war with these innocent people, living peaceably at home, and doing injury to none, which was the ruin of a great number of them. Now, because this region affords no gold; and if it did the inhabitants would soon have wrought away their lives by hard working in the mines, that so he might accumulate gold by their bodies and souls, for which Christ was crucified: for the generality he made slaves of those whose lives he spared, and sent away such ships as were driven thither by the wind of report, loaden with them, exchanging them for wine, oil, vinegar, salt pork, garments, pack horses and other commodities, which he thought most necessary and fit for his use. He proposed to them the choice of fifty virgins, and she that was the fairest or best complexioned he bartered for a small cask of wine, oil, vinegar or some inconsiderable quantity of salt pork, the same exchange he preferred of two or three

---

[47] Francisco de Montejo conquered much of the Yucatán Peninsula. His son (also named Francisco) founded Mérida in 1542.

hundred well-disposed young boys, and one of them who had the mind or presence of a prince's son, was given up to them for a cheese, and one hundred more for a horse. Thus he continued his flagitious courses from 1526 to 1533, inclusively, till there was news brought of the wealth and opulence of the region of Perú, whither the Spaniards marched, and so for some time there was a cessation of this tyranny; but in a few days after they returned and acted enormous crimes, robbed, and imprisoned them and committed higher offences against the God of Heaven; nor have they ye done, so that now these three hundred leagues of land so populous (as I said before) lies now uncultivated and almost deserted.

No solifidian can believe the particular narrations of their barbarism, and cruelty in those countries. I will only relate two or three stories which are fresh in my memory. The Spaniards used to trace the steps of the Indians, both men and women with furious dogs. An Indian woman that was sick, who perceiving that she was not able to avoid being torn in pieces by the dogs, took a rope and tied a boy who was one year old to her foot and hanged herself from a beam. And she did not do it so quickly that the dogs did not arrive and tore the boy apart, although he was baptized by a friar just before he had died.

Illustration 14: De Bry, Theodor, ca. 1598. Infant dismemberment to feed dogs. On: Brevíssima relación de la destruyción de las Indias. Frankfurt, 1598. 3D image on http://bit.ly/casas14.

When the Spaniards left this kingdom, one of them invited the son of some Indian governor of a city or province, to go along with him, who told him he would not leave or desert his native country. The Spaniard threatened to cut off his ears, if he refused to follow him. But the youth persisted resolutely, that he would stay in the place of his nativity. Then the Spaniard drawing his sword cut off each ear, and then as if he had only pinched him, smilingly cut off his nose and lips. This rogue did lasciviously boast before a priest, and as if he had merited the greatest applause, commended himself to the very heavens, saying, "he had made it his chief trade or business to impregnate Indian women, so that he would get more money from the them when they were sold."

In this kingdom (or in some province of New Spain), a certain Spaniard hunting and intent on his game, fancied that his beagles wanted food; and to supply their hunger snatched a young little babe from the mother's breast, cutting off his arms and legs, cast a part of them to every dog, which they devoured, then he threw the remainder of the body to them. Thus, it is plainly manifest how they value these poor creatures, created after the image of God. What follows is (if possible) a sin of a deeper dye.

Those haughty obdurate and execrable tyrants, who departed from this country to fish for riches in Perú, and four monks of the Order of St. Francis, with Father Jacob[48] who travelled thither also to appease, preach, and bring Jesus Christ to the remaining people of the infernal vintage and tyrannical massacres that the Spaniards had perpetrated in seven years. I think it was these religious who sent the messengers to the Indians in the thirty-fourth year to see if they had any good sense that they would enter their lands to tell them of only one God who was the true Lord of the whole world. They entered council and made many town halls. They first took a lot of information about what men were those who claimed to be fathers and friars, what they intended, how they differed from the Christians from whom so many grievances and injustices had received. Finally, they agreed to receive them, with which only they, and not Spaniards, entered. The religious men promised it because the viceroy of New Spain had granted it, and they were promised that Spaniards would not enter there, but religious men.

They preached the gospel of Christ (as they usually do) and the holy intention of the Kings of Spain to them. So much love and flavor they took with the doctrine and example of the friars, and so much they lavished on the news of the kings of Castile (of which in all the past seven years the Spaniards never gave them the news that they had another king, but he who tyrannized and destroyed them there), that after forty days that the friars had entered and preached, the lords of the land brought them and gave all their idols to burn them, and after this their children to teach, that they love them more than the lights of their eyes, and they made them churches and temples and houses, and invited them from other provinces to go to preach to them and to give them news of God and of those who said he was the great King of Castile.

And persuaded of the friars, they did one thing that was never done in the Indies until today, and all those who pretend to be some of the tyrants who have destroyed those kingdoms and great lands there are falsehoods and lies. Twelve or fifteen lords of many vassals and lands each by themselves,

---

[48] Jacobo de Tastera (or Testera).

gathering their peoples and taking their votes and consent, were subject of their own will to the lordship of the kings of Castile, receiving the Emperor, as King of Spain, by supreme lord and universal, and signs such as signatures were successful, which I have in my possession with the testimony of the friars.

While the friars were having joy and hope to bring Jesus Christ to all the people of that kingdom, there came to their lands 18 Spaniards pulled by horse and 12 on foot and brought many loads of idols taken from other provinces to the Indians. The Captain of the said 30 Spaniards called a lord of the land where they entered and tells him to take those idol charges and distribute them throughout his land. Each idol would be sold at the cost of an Indian to make him a slave, threatening him that if he did not, he would make war on him. The said lord, out of forced fear, distributed the idols throughout his land, and sent all his vassals to take them to worship them and give him Indians to give them to the Spaniards as slaves. The Indians who had two children gave one, and who had three gave two, and in this way they fulfilled that sacrilegious trade, and the lord or Cacique pleased the Spaniards.

One of these hellish unholy thieves, named Juan García, being sick and propincuous to death, had under his bed two loads of idols, and sent an Indian who served him to look well that those idols who were there did not give them to barter of chickens because they were very good at exchanging each for a slave. With this will, and in this care, the wretched man died, and who doubts that he is not in the buried hells. See and consider what is the use, religion, examples of Christianity of the Spaniards who go to the Indies, what honor they seek God, how they work so that God is known and worshiped of those people, how careful they are to sow, grow, and expand their holy faith. Judge if it was a minor sin, than that of Jeroboam, who would fecit Israel making the two golden calves for the people to worship, or if it was the same as Judas, or that more scandal caused it. These are the works of the Spaniards who go to the Indies, who for the greed they have for gold, sell, and deny Jesus Christ.

The Indians, seeing that the promise had not been fulfilled that Spaniards were not to enter those provinces, and that the Spaniards themselves brought idols from other lands to sell, having given all their gods to the friars to burn them for worship a true God, they get uprooted and outraged. They went to the friars to claim them, "why did you lie to us, saying that Christians were not to enter this land? Why did they burn our gods, if Christians are going to come to sell the gods of other provinces? Weren't our gods better than those of other nations?" The religious placated them as best they could, having nothing to answer.

They went to find the 30 Spaniards and told them the damage they had done. They were asked to leave and they didn't want to. Before that, the Spaniards made the Indians believe that the same friars were the ones who had brought him there, that it was consummated malice. The Indians agreed to kill the friars; and these fled because certain Indians warned them. After the friars left, the Indians realized the innocence and virtue of the friars, and the evil of the Spaniards. They sent messengers fifty leagues behind them, begging them to turn and asking for forgiveness of the alteration they caused them. The religious, as servants of God and jealous of those souls, returned to land and were received as angels. The Indians did a thousand services, and the friars stayed there for an additional four or five months.

In the meantime, those Christians never wanted to leave the land, nor could the Viceroy[49] take them out (because he was far from New Spain, and although he made them apologize for traitors). Because they did not cease to make their customary insults and grievances to the Indians, it seemed to the religious that late or early with such bad deeds the Indians would slip and perhaps fall on them. Especially, that they could not preach to the Indians with their stillness and theirs and without continuous shocks, by the bad works of the Spaniards, they agreed to forsake that kingdom, and thus it was left without fire and help of doctrine.

Those souls were left in the darkness of ignorance and misery that they were, taking away at the best time the remedy and irrigation of the news and knowledge of God, which they were already taking eagerly, as if we were taking the water from the newly laid plants. And this because of the inexpiable guilt and evil consumed by those Spaniards.

---

[49] Antonio de Mendoza.

OF THE PROVINCE OF ST. MARTHA

http://bit.ly/mar-brief

In the province of Santa Marta[50], the Indians had a lot of gold because the land was rich and the regions had the industry to take it. For this reason, from the year of 1498 until today, the year of 1542, something else has not made infinite Spanish tyrants but to travel there with ships to jump, kill, and steal the gold from the people.

Since 1523, several captains succeeded each other, some more cruel than others. Each one made the profession of doing more exorbitant cruelties and evils than the other, because the rule we mentioned earlier would be true. A great tyrant was in 1529, with purpose and many people. Without fear of God or compassion of human lineage, he made such great ravages, massacres and impieties that he exceeded all past.

Between him and those who accompanied him they stole many treasures in the span of six or seven years that they lived there. After he died (without confession), and even fleeing from the residence he had, other killer tyrants and robbers succeeded who were consuming the remaining people than from the hands and cruel knife of the past.

They spread so much inland ravaging large and many provinces, killing, captivating people, giving great torments to lords and vassals, because they discovered gold and peoples. From the said year of 1529 until today they have depopulated more than four hundred leagues of land, which was thus populated like the others.

I truly affirm that I would have to tell a very long story about the evils, massacres, depopulations, injustices, violence, ravages and great sins that the Spaniards did in these kingdoms of Santa Marta and committed against God, the King, and the innocent people, but This stays for your time, if God allows it. I just want to say a few words of which the King our lord the Bishop of that province now describes, who wrote on May 20, 1541 and read:

---

[50] Santa Martha was located in what is now the Republic of Colombia.

"I must acquaint your Sacred Majesty, that the only way to succor and support this tottering region is to free it from the power of a father in law, and marry it to a husband who will treat her as she ought to be, and lovingly entertain her, and that must be done with all possible expedition too. If not, I am certain that she will suddenly decay and come to nothing by the covetous and sordid deportment of the governors, &c." He adds, "and this I will make appear to your Majesty that they are not Christians, but devils; not servants of God and the King, but traitors to the King and laws, who are conversant in those regions. And in reality nothing can be more obstructive to those that live peaceably, then inhumane and barbarous usage, which they, who lead a quiet and peaceable life, too frequently undergo, and this is so fastidious and nauseous to them, that there can be nothing in the world so odious and detestable among them, as the name of a Christian: for they term the Christians in their language *yares*, that is, devils; and in truth are not without reason; for the actions of those that reside in these regions, are not such as speak them to be Christians or men, gifted with reason, but absolute devils. Hence it is, that Indians, perceiving these actions committed by the heads as well as members, who are void of all compassion and humanity, do judge the Christian laws to be of the same strain and temper, and that their God and King are the authors of such enormities. As the Indians see this evil work and without mercy, they think that this is the law of the Christians, and the author is God and his king. To persuade them of something else, is to want to deplete the sea, to give them matter of laughing, mocking, and derision of the law of Jesus Christ. As the Indian warriors see this treatment that is done to the Pacific, they prefer to die at once, before many at the hands of Spaniards. Only this, unbeaten Caesar, from experience, &c.." And he adds further, "Your Majesty has more servants here than you think, because there are soldiers publicly saying that when they assault, steal, destroy, kill, or burn Your Majesty's vassals to obtain gold, it is because it serves Your Majesty. And therefore, it would be good, Christian Caesar, that Your Majesty would give them to understand, punishing some rigorously, that he does not receive service when God is not being served."

All of the above are formal words of the Bishop of Santa Marta, which will clearly show what is done in all those unfortunate lands and against those innocent people. The Indian warriors have been saved by fleeing the massacres of the Spaniards by the mountains, and the Pacific are placed in the tyrannical and horrible servitude. In the mountains, when the Indians who carry heavy loads fall or faint from weakness and work, the Spaniards kick them, give sticks, and break their teeth with the handles of the swords so that they get up and walk unresolved. They usually say, "Oh, you're bad! I can't anymore. Kill me here. I want to be dead here." And they say this with great sighs and chest tightness, showing great anguish and pain. Oh, who could imply a hundredth part of the afflictions and calamities that those innocent people suffer! Blessed is he who makes understand those who can and should remedy it.

OF THE PROVINCE OF CARTAGENA

 (included in previous recording)

This Province is distant fifty leagues from the Isle of St. Martha Westward, and situated on the confines of the province of Cenú, from whence it extends one hundred leagues to the bay of Urabá, and contains a very long tract of land Southward. From the year 1498 to this present time, these provinces were most barbarously used, and made desert by murder and slaughter. To conclude soon this brief summary, I will not handle the particulars, but to refer to the evils that are done in others now.[51]

---

[51] Some of the conquerors in this area were Juan de la Cosa, Cristóbal Guerra, Alonso de Hojeda and Diego de Nicuesa.

OF THE PERL COAST, PARIA AND THE TRINIDAD ISLE

🎧 http://bit.ly/per-brief

The Spaniards made great spoils and havoc from the Paria[52] coast to the bay of Venezuela, exclusively, which is about two hundred leagues. It can hardly be expressed by tongue or pen how many, and how great injuries and injustices, the inhabitants of this seashore have endured from the year 1510, to this day. I will only relate two or three peculiar and criminal acts of the first magnitude, capable of comprehending all other enormities that deserve the sharpest torments, wit and malice can invent, and so make way for a deserved judgment upon them.

The Trinidad Isle exceeds Sicile, both in amplitude and fertility, and is contiguous to the continent on that side where it touches upon Paria (whose inhabitants, according to their quality, are more addicted to probity and virtue, than the rest of the Indians). In 1510, A nameless pirate[53], accompanied with a parcel of sixty or seventy, arrived and published an edict, that all the inhabitants should come and cohabit with them. The Indian lords and subjects gave them a debonair and brotherly reception, serving them with wonderful alacrity, furnishing them with daily provisions in so plentiful a manner, that they might have sufficed a more numerous company; for it is the mode among Indians of this new world, to supply the Spaniards very generously with all manner of necessaries. A short time after the Spaniards came, they built a stately house, which was going to be an apartment for the Indians (so that they could eventually accomplish A premeditated design). When they were to thatch it, and had been raised two men's height, they enclosed several Indians there, to expedite the work, as they pretended. Then, some of the Spaniards surrounded the house with swords in hand so

---

[52] Paria and the Pearl Coast refer together to what is today known as the Paria Peninsula, in Northeast Venezuela. The pearl-fishing was conducted in the waters around Isla Margarita.

[53] Juan Bono, a Basque.

that no one should would come out, and others inside bound the Indians, menacing them with death, if they offered to move afoot. The Spaniards menaced that, if any one endeavored to escape, he was going to be cut in pieces. Some of the Indians who escaped, wounded and healthy, and others from the town who had not entered, took their bows and arrows, and gathered to another house of the town to defend themselves, where a hundred or two hundred of them entered; and defending the door, the Spaniards burned down the house and everyone alive.

From here, they set sail to the island of San Juan with about 188 slaves, whom they had bound, where they sold half of them. Then they went to Hispaniola, where they disposed of the rest. Now when I reprehended this captain about this betrayal in the very isle of San Juan, he dismissed me with this answer: "Forbear good Sir. I had this in commission from those who sent me, that I should surprise them by the spetious pretense of peace, whom I could not seize by open force." In truth, this same captain told me with his own mouth, that in all his life he had found neither father nor mother, but on the island of the Trinity, according to the good works that the Indians had done to him.

The monks of our order of St. Dominic held a consult about sending one of their fraternity into this island. They sent a religious graduate in theology, of great virtue and holiness, with a lay friar as a companion[54], to see the earth, treat people, and find a suitable place to make monasteries. When the religious arrived, the Indians received them as angels from heaven, and heard them with great affection, attention, and joy the words they could understand (more by signs than by speech, because they did not know the language).

It happened that, after the departure of that vessel that brought these religious men, another came into the port, whose crew according to their hellish custom, fraudulently, and unknown to the religious took away a Prince of that province as captive, who was called Alfonso (Indians are friends and greedy to have a Christian's name, and then ask him to give it to him, even before they know anything about being baptized). The said lord Alfonso was deceitfully over persuaded to go on board with his wife and

---

[54] Francisco Hernández de Córdoba was Antonio Montesino's companion.

about seventeen more, pretending that they would give them a party; which the prince and they believed, for he was confident, that the religious would by no means suffer him or be abused, for he had no so much confidence in the Spaniards; but as soon as they were upon deck, the perfidious rogues, set sail for Hispaniola, where they were sold as slaves.

The whole country being extremely discomposed and understanding that their prince and princess were violently carried away, addressed themselves to these clergymen, who were in great danger of losing their lives. But they were extraordinarily afflicted, and probably would have suffered death, rather than permit the Indians to be so injuriously dealt with, which might prove an obstruction to their receiving of, and believing in God's word. Yet the Indians were sedated by the promises of the religious; for they told them, they would send letters by the first ship that was bound for Hispaniola, whereby they would procure the restitution and return of their lord and his retinue. It pleased God to send a ship thither forthwith, to the greater confirming of the governor's damnation, where in the letters they sent to the religious of Hispaniola, letters containing repeated exclamations and protestations, and protest against such actions. But those that received them denied them justice, for that they were partakers of that prey, made of those Indians so unjustly and impiously captivated. But the religious, who had promised the inhabitants, that their Lord Alfonso should be back within four months, and found that neither in four, nor eight months he was returned, they prepared themselves for death, and to deliver up their life to Christ, to whom they had offered it before their departure from Spain: Thus the innocent Indians were revenged on the innocent priests; for they were of opinion, that the religious had a hand in the plot, partly, because they found their promises that their lord should return within four months, ineffectual, and partly because the inhabitants made no difference between a religious friar and a Spanish rogue. At another time it fell out likewise, through the rampant tyranny and cruel deeds of evil-minded Christians, that the Indians put to death two Dominican friars, of which I am a faithful witness, escaping myself, not without a very great miracle, which transaction I resolve silently to pass over, lest I should terrify the reader with the horror of the fact.

In these provinces, there was a city seated on the Bay of Codera, whose lord was called Higueroto, a name, either proper to persons or common to the rulers of that place. A Cacique with such clemency, and his subjects of such noted virtue, that the Spaniards who came thither, were extraordinarily welcome, furnished with provisions, enjoying peace and comfort, and no refreshment wanting. But a perfidious wretch got many of them onboard and sold them to the islanders of San Juan. At the same time, I landed upon that island, where I obtained a sight of this tyrant, and heard the relation of his actions. He utterly destroyed that land, which the rest of the Spaniards took very unkindly at his hands, who frequently played the pirate, and robbed on that shore, detesting it as a wicked thing, because they had lost that place, where they use to be treated with as great hospitality and freedom, as if they had been under their own roof. Nay they transported from this place, among them, to the Isles of Hispaniola and San Juan two million men and upward and made the coast a desert.

It is most certainly true, that they never ship off a vessel freighted with Indians, but they pay a third part as tribute to the sea, besides those who are slaughter, when found in their own houses. Now the source and original of all this is the ends they have proposed to themselves. For there is a necessity of taking with them a great number of Indians, that they may gain a great sum of money by their sale, now the ships are very slenderly furnished with provisions and water in small quantity, to satisfy few, left the tyrants, who are termed owners or proprietors of ships should be at too great expense in victualling their vessels, nay they scarce carry food enough with them to maintain the Spaniards that manage the vessel, which is the reason so many *Indians* dye with hunger and thirst, and of necessity they must be thrown over-board: Nay one of them told me this for a truth, that there being such a multitude of men thus destroyed, a ship may sail from the Isle of Lucaya to Hispaniola, which is a voyage of twenty leagues and upward, without chart or compass, by the sole direction or observation of dead floating bodies.

But afterward, when arrived, and driven up into the Isle whither they are brought to be sold, there is no person that is in some small measure compassionate, but would be extremely moved and discomposed at the sight; *viz.* to spy old men and women, together with naked children half starved. Then they separate parents from children, wives from their husbands, about ten or twenty in a company, and cast lots for them, that the detestable owners of the ships may have their share; who prepare two or three ships, and equip them as a fleet of pirates, going ashore ravaging and forcing men out of their houses, and then robbing them: But when the lot of any one of them falls upon a parcel, that hath an aged or diseased man; the tyrant, whose allotment he is, usually bursts out, as followed. "Let this old fellow be dammed, why do you bestow him upon me; must I, think you; be at the charge of his burial? And this sickly wretch, how must I take care for his cure?" Hence, you may guess what estimate and value the Spaniards put upon Indians, and whether they practice and fulfill that divine and heavenly precept enjoying mutual love and society.

There can be nothing crueler and detestable then the tyrannical use of the Indians in pearl-fishing There is no hellish and desperate life in this century that can be compared, although the gold in the mines is in its very serious and lousy genre. They put them in the sea in three, four and five deep fathoms; from the morning until the sun goes down they are always underwater, swimming without resounding, plucking the oysters where the pearls are raised. They leave with some nets filled to the top, and to solve, where is a Spanish executioner in a canoe or wafer, and if they take time to rest, he gives them handfuls and throws them into the water to turn them to fish. Their food is fish, and the meat which is contained within the oysters, *cassava* made of roots with a few *mahids*, the bread of that country. In the former there is little or no nutriment or substance, and the other is not made without great trouble, of which they never get fed up. Their lodging or bed is the earth confined to a pair of stocks, for fear that they should run away. It frequently happens that they are drowned with the toil of this kind of fishing and never more seen, for the *tuberoms* and *maroxi* (certain marine monsters that devour a complete proportioned man wholly at once) prey upon them under water. You must consider withall, that it is impossible for the strongest constitution to continue long under water without breathing, and they ordinarily dye through the extreme rigor of the cold, spitting blood which is occasioned by the too great compression of the breast, procreated by a continued holding breath under water, for by too much cold a profluvium of blood follows. Their hair naturally black is changed into a combust, burnt or sun-color like that of the sea wolves, their shoulders and backs covered, or overspread with a saltish humor that they appear rather like monsters in humane shape than men.

They have destroyed all the Lucayans by this intolerable or rather diabolical exercise, for the customary emolument or gain of lucre, and by this means gained the value of fifty, sometime one hundred castelians of every individual Indian. They sell them (though it is prohibited) publicly, for the Lucayans were excellent swimmers, and several perished in this isle that came from other provinces.

OF THE RIVER YUPARI

http://bit.ly/yup-brief

A river called Yupari rises upland over two hundred leagues. Through it, a sad tyrant rose many leagues the year of 1529 with four 400 or more men, and made great slaughters, burning alive and blaming innocent infinities that were in their lands and houses without doing any harm to anyone, neglected, and left very large amount of land scorched and astonished and chased away. Finally, he ha a bad death and his army broke down, then other tyrants succeeded in those evils and tyrannies, and today they go around destroying and killing and inferring the souls redeemed with the Son of God's blood.

OF THE KINGDOM OF VENEZUELA

http://bit.ly/ven-brief

O ur Sovereign Lord the King in the year 1526, over-persuaded by fallacious appearances (for the Spaniards use to conceal from His Majesties knowledge the damages and detriments, which God himself, the souls and state of the Indians did suffer) entrusted the kingdom of Venezuela longer and larger than the Spanish dominions, with its government and absolute jurisdiction to some German merchants, with power to make certain capitulations and conventions, who came into this kingdom with 300, and there found a benign mild and peaceable people, as they were throughout the Indies till injured by the Spaniards. These more cruel then the rest beyond comparison, behaved themselves more inhumanely then rapacious tigers, wolves and lions, for they had the jurisdiction of this kingdom, and therefore possessing it with the greater freedom from control; lay in wait and were the more vigilant with greater care and avarice to understand the practical part of heaping up wealth, and robbing the inhabitants of their gold and silver, surpassing all their predecessors in those indirect ways, rejecting wholly both the fear of their God and King, nay forgetting that they were born men with reasonable faculties.

These incarnate devils laid waste and desolated 400 leagues of most fertile land, containing vast and wonderful provinces, most spacious and large valleys surrounded with hills, 40 leagues in length, and many towns richly abounding in gold and silver. They destroyed so many and such considerable regions, that there is not one supernumerary witness left to relate the story, if they are not some who will have gotten into the caverns and bowels of the earth, fleeing from such a strange and pestilential knife. I judge that they by new invented and unusual torments ruined four or five million souls and sent them all to hell. I will give a taste of two or three of their transactions, that hereby you may guess at the rest.

They seized the supreme lord of the whole province without any cause whatsoever of drawing gold by tormenting him. He broke loose, ran away, and went to the mountains. All the people of the land were uprooted and frightened, hiding in the mountains and rocks. The Spaniards went looking for them, found them and made cruel massacres and all those who took them alive were sold as slaves in public places.

They seized the supreme lord of the whole province without cause than to extract gold by tormenting him. He broke loose, ran away, and went to the mountains. All the people of the land were uprooted and frightened, hiding in the mountains and rocks. The Spaniards went looking for them, found them and made cruel massacres and all those who took them alive were sold as slaves in public lunches.

In all the provinces they came to, before they caught the main lord, they were greeted with songs, dances, and many gold presents in large numbers. The payment they were given, for sowing fear in all that land, was to put them in the sword and break them up. Once, after receiving them in the said manner, the German captain ordered that many people be put in a straw house to tear them apart. As the house had beams at the top, many people climbed into them, to flee the bloody hands of those men and their swords.

The infernal man sent fire to the house, where all who were left were burned alive. A large number of towns were depopulated by this cause, all people fleeing through the mountains, where they planned to save themselves.

Illustration 15: The Indians received Spaniards with presents, and the payment they gave them was the sword and tearing them apart [engraving]. On: Brevissima relación de la destruyción de las Indias. Frankfurt, 1598. 3D image on **http://bit.ly/lascasas15***.*

They arrived at another large province in the confines of Santa Marta. They found Indians in their homes, in their peaceful and occupied villages and estates. They spent a lot of time with them eating their food and the Indians serving them as if they were to give them their lives and their salvation. The Indians suffered their continuous oppressions and ordinary importunities, which were intolerable. A single Spaniard ate in one day what ten Indians ate in a month.

During that time, the Indians gave them a lot of gold of their own will, with countless other good works. When the tyrants wanted to leave, they agreed to pay their attention in this way: the German tyrant (and also, to what we believe, heretic, because he neither heard mass nor allowed others to participate, with other signs of Lutheran[55] who were known) ordered all the Indians to be arrested with their wives and children. They put them in a large pen that was made for the purpose. He let them know that whoever wanted to go out and be free had to give so much gold for himself, his wife and for each child. To push them further, he ordered that they not be given food until they brought him the gold he was asking for their rescue. Many sought gold for their rescue, as they could. They were released and returned to their farmhouses and houses to make their food. Then the tyrant sent Spanish thieves to catch the same Indians again. They were taken to the corral, given them the torment of hunger and thirst again until they were rescued again. Some Indians were arrested and rescued many times. Others could not be rescued because they had already given all the gold they owned. He left those in the pen to perish until they died of hunger. In this way, this rich province of people and gold was left desolated and depopulated, which had a valley of forty leagues, and in it burned a town that had 1,000 houses.

Furthermore, this tyrant was big with an itching desire after the discovery of the Perusian mines, which he did accomplish. Nay should I enumerate the particular cruelties, slaughters, &c. committed by him though my discourse would not in the least be contrarian to the truth, yet it would not be believed and only stupefied and amaze the reader.

He agreed this infernal tyrant to go inland with greed and eagerness to discover the hell of Perú. For this unhappy journey he took him and the other infinite Indians loaded with loads between 90 and 130 pounds, strung on chains. If one got tired or fainted from hunger, work, and weakness; then they cut off his head through the chain's collar, for not stopping to disassemble the others that were in the outermost collars; and the head fell to one part and the body to another, and they distributed the load of the latter over those carried by the others. Saying the provinces that ravaged, the cities and places that burned (because they are all the straw houses), the people that killed, the cruelties that in particular killings perpetrated on that road, is not credible, but frightening and true.

------

[55] The term was used at the time to indicate any deviant from the Catholic religion orthodoxy.

This course the other tyrants took who set sail from Venezuela and St. Martha (with the same resolution of detecting the Perusian golden, consecrated houses as them they esteemed) who found the fruitful region so desolate, deserted, and wasted by fire and sword, that those cruel tyrants themselves were smitten with wonder and astonishment at the traces and ruins of such prodigious devastations.

All these things and many more were proved by witnesses in the Council of the Indians, and the records of their testimony were entered in that court, though these execrable tyrants burnt many of them that there might be little or nothing proved as a cause of those great devastations and evils perpetrated by them.

For the ministers of justice who have hitherto lived the Indies, through their obscure and damnable blindness, were not much solicitous about the punishment of the crimes and butcheries which have been and are still committed by these tyrants. They may only say "possibly because so and so had wickedly and barbarously dealt with the Indians, that is the reason why thousands of castelians have been lost from his majesties annual revenue," and this general and confused proof is sufficient (as they worthily conceive) to purge or repress such great and heinous crimes.

And even this they do not know how to find out, nor do nor make them more expensive, because if they did what they owe to God and the King, they would find that the said German tyrants have robbed the King of 3 million gold Castilians, because those provinces of Venezuela, with the ones that have ravaged the most, ravaged and depopulated through 400 leagues, is the richest and most prosperous land of gold and era of population in the world. And more income has hindered and spoiled the kings of Spain of that kingdom of 2 million in 16 years that the enemy tyrants of God and the King began to destroy. And these damages from here to the end of the world there is no hope of being recovered, if God did not do it by miracle to resurrect so many tales of dead souls. These are the temporary damages of the King; It would be well to consider how such and how many are the damages, dishonors, blasphemies, infamies of God and his law, and how many innumerable souls will be rewarded as they are burning in hell for the greed and inhumanity of these animal or German tyrants.

But, I will conclude that from the time they entered upon this country to this very day, that is, 17 years, they have remitted many ships freighted with Indians to be sold as slaves to the isles of St. Martha, Hispaniola, Jamaica, and San Juan, selling a million of persons at the least. I speak modestly, and still do expose to this very year of our lord 1542, the King's council in this island seeing and knowing it, permit and countenance, and wink at the horrid impieties and devastations which are committed on the coasts of this continent, extending 400 leagues in length, and continues still together with Venezuela and St. Martha under their jurisdiction, which they could had easily remedied and timely prevented.

OF THE PROVINCES OF FLORIDA

 http://bit.ly/flo-brief

Three tyrants at several times made their entrance into these provinces since the year 1510, or 1511, to act those crimes which others. Two of these[56] three made it their sole business to do in other regions, to the end, that they might advance themselves to higher dignities and promotions than they could deserve, by the effusion of blood and destruction of these people. But at length they all were cut off by a violent death, and the houses which they formerly built and erected with the cement of human blood, (which I can sufficiently testified of these three) perished with them, and their memory rotten, and as absolutely washed away from off the face of the earth, as if they had never had a being. These men deserted these regions, leaving them in great distraction and confusion, nor were they branded with less notes of infamy, by the certain slaughters they perpetrated, though they were but few in number than the rest. For the just God cut them off before they did much mischief and reserved the castigation and revenge of those evils which I know, and was an eyewitness of, to this very time and place. As to the fourth tyrant[57], who lately, that is, in the year 1538, came hither well-furnished with men and ammunition, we have received no

---

[56] Possibly Ponce de León and Pánfilo de Narváez.

[57] Hernando de Soto.

account these three years last past; but we are very confident, that he, at his first arrival, acted like a bloody tyrant, even to ecstasy and madness, if he be still alive with his follower, and did injure, destroy, and consume a vast number of men (for he was branded with infamous cruelty above all those who with their assistants committed crimes and enormities of the first magnitude in these kingdoms and provinces) I conceive, God hath punished him with the same violent death, as he did other tyrants: But because my pen is wearied with relating such execrable and sanguinary deeds (not of men but beasts) I will trouble myself no longer with the dismal and fatal consequences thereof.

These people were found by them to be wise, grave, and well disposed, though their usual butcheries and cruelties in oppressing them like brutes, with heavy burthens, did rack their minds with great terror and anguish. At their entry into a certain village, they were welcomed with great joy and exultation, replenished them with victuals, till they were all satisfied, yielding up to them above 600 men to carry their bag and baggage, and like grooms to look after their horses: The Spaniards departing thence, a captain related to the superior tyrant returned thither to rob this (no ways diffident or mistrustful) people, and pierced their King through with a lance, of which wound he dyed upon the spot, and committed several other cruelties into the bargain. In another neighboring town, whose inhabitants they thought, were more vigilant and watchful, having had the news of their horrid acts and deeds, they barbarously murdered them all with their lances and swords, destroying all, young and old, great and small, lords and subject without exception.

The chief tyrant caused many Indians (above two hundred as 'tis noised abroad) whom he summoned to appear before him out of another town, or else, who came voluntarily to pay their respects to him, to have their noses and lips to the very beard, cut off; and thus in this grievous and wretched condition, the blood gushing out of their wounds, returned them back, to give an infallible testimony of the works and miracles wrought by these preachers and ministers baptized in the Catholic faith.

Now let all men judge what affection and love they bear to Christianity; to what purpose, or upon what account they believe there is a God, whom they preach and boast of to be good and just, and that his law which they profess (and indeed only profess) to be pure and immaculate. The mischiefs acted by these profligate wretches and sons of perdition were of the deepest die. At last this captain devoted to perdition dyed impenitent, nor do we in the least question, but that he is overwhelmed and buried in darkness infernal, unless God according to his infinite mercy and boundless clemency, not his own merits, (he being contaminated and poisoned with execrable deeds) be pleased to compassionate and have mercy upon him.

OF THE PLATE RIVER, THAT IS, RÍO DEL LA PLATA

 http://bit.ly/rio-brief

Some captains[58] since the year 1502 to 1503 undertook four or five voyages to the River of Plate, which embrace within its own arms great kingdoms and provinces, and is peopled by rational and well-tempered inhabitants. In the general we are certified, that they were very injurious and bloody to them; but being far distant from those Indians, we frequently discourse of, we are not able to give you a particular account of their transactions. Yet beyond all controversies, they did, and still do go the same way to work, as others in several regions to this present time do, and have done; for they are the same, (and many in number too) Spaniards who went thither, that were the wicked instruments of other executions, and all of them aim at one and the same thing, namely to grow rich and wealthy, which they can never be, unless they steer the same course which others have followed, and tread the same paths in murdering, robbing and destroying poor Indians.

After I had committed to writing what I have aforementioned, it was told me for a great truth, that they had laid waste in those countries great kingdoms and provinces, dealing cruelly and bloodily with these harmless people, at a horrid rate, having a greater opportunity and convenience to be

---

[58] The region was discovered in 1515 by Díaz de Solís. Others in charge of expeditions were Sebastián Cabot, Pedro de Mendoza, Martínez de Irala, Juan de Ayolas, and Álvar Núñez Cabeza de Vaca.

more infamous and rigid to them, then others, they being very remote from Spain, living inordinately, like debauches, laying aside, and bidding farewell to all manner of justice, which is indeed a stranger in all the American regions, as is manifest by what hath been said already. But among the other numerous wicked acts following this is one that may be read in the Indians Courts. One of the governors commanded his soldiers to go to a certain village, and if they denied them provisions, to put all the inhabitants to the sword: By virtue of this authority away they march, and because they would not yield to them above five thousand men as enemies, fearing rather to be seen, then guilty of illiberality, were cut off by the sword.

Also a certain number of men living in peace and tranquility proffered their services to him; who, as it fell out, were called before the governor, but deferring their appearance a little longer than ordinary, that he might infix their minds with a remark of horrible tyranny, he commanded, they should be delivered up, as prisoners to their mortal Indian enemies, who begged with loud clamors and a deluge of tears, that they might be dispatched out of this world by their own hands, rather than be given up as a prey to the enemy; yet being resolute, they would not depart out of the house wherein they were, so the Spaniards hacked them in pieces limb by limb, who exclaimed and cried aloud, "We came to visit and serve you peaceably and quietly, and you murder us; our blood with which these walls are moistened and sprinkled will remain as an everlasting testimony of our unjust slaughter, and your barbarous cruelty." And really this *Piaculum* or horrid crime deserves a commemoration, or rather speak more properly, the commiseration of all persons.

OF THE VAST KINGDOMS AND SPACIOUS PROVINCES OF PERÚ

http://bit.ly/gra-brief

A notorious tyrant[59] in the year 1531, entered the kingdoms of *Perú* with his accomplices, upon the same account, and with the same pretenses, and beginning at the same rate as others did; he indeed being one of those who were exercised, and highly concerned in the slaughters and cruelties committed on the continent ever since the year 1510, he increased and heightened the cruelties, butcheries, and rapine; destroying and laying waste (being a false-hearted faithless person) the towns and villages, and murdering the inhabitants, which occasioned all those evils, that succeeded in those regions afterward. Now, to undertake the writing of a narrative of them, and represent them lively and naturally to the readers view, and perusal, is a work altogether impossible, but must lie concealed and unknown until they shall more openly and clearly appear, and be made visible to every eye, at the day of judgment. As for my part, if I should presume to unravel, in some, measure the deformity, quality and circumstances of those enormities, I must ingenuously confess I could by no means perform so burdensome a task, and render it complete and as it ought to be.

At his first admission into these parts, he had laid waste some towers, and robbed them of a great quantity of gold, this he did in the infancy of his tyrannical attempts, when he arrived at Puná a neighboring isle so called, he had the reception of an angel; but about six months after, when the Spaniards had spent all their provisions, they discovered and opened the Indians stores and granaries, which were laid up for the sustenance of themselves, wives and children against a time of dearth and scarcity, brought them forth with tears and weepings, to dispose of at pleasure: But they rewarded them with slaughter, slavery and depopulation as formerly.

Thence they betook themselves to the Tumbala province, situated on the firm land, where they put to death all they met with. And because the people terrified with their abominable sins of commission, fled from their

---

[59] Francisco Pizarro.

cruelty, they were accused of rebellion against the Spanish King. This tyrant made use of this artifice, he commanded all that he took, or that had bestowed gold, silver and other rich gifts on him, still to load him with other presents, till he found they had exhausted their treasures, and were grown naked and incapable of affording him farther supplies, and then he declared them to be the vassals and subjects of the King of Spain, flattering them, and proclaiming twice by sound of trumpet, that for the future he would not captivate or molest them anymore, looking upon it as lawful to rob, and terrify them with such messages as he had done, before he admitted them under the King's protection, as if from that very time, he had never robbed, destroyed or oppressed them with tyrannical usage.

Not long after Ataliba the King and Supreme Emperor of all these kingdoms, leading a great number of naked men, he himself being at the head of them, armed with ridiculous weapons, and wholly ignorant of the goodness of the *Spaniards* Bilbo-Blades, the mortal dartings of their lances, and the strength of their horse, whose use and service was to him altogether unknown, and never so much as heard of before, and that the Spaniards were sufficiently weaponed to rob the devils themselves of gold, if they had any, came to the place where they then were; saying, "Where are these Spaniards? Let them appear, I will not stir a foot from hence till they give me satisfaction for my subjects whom they have slain, my towns they have reduced to ashes, and my riches they have stolen from me." The Spaniards meet him, make a great slaughter of his men, and seize on the person of the King himself, who was carried in a chair or sedan on men's shoulders. There was a treaty had about his redemption, the King engaged to lay down four millions of castelians, as the purchase of his freedom, but fifteen were paid down upon the nail: They promise to set him at liberty, but contrary to all faith and truth according to their common custom (for they always violated their promises with the Indians) they falsely imposed this upon him, that his people were got together in a body by his command; but the King was made answer, that throughout his dominions, not so much as a leaf upon a tree durst move without his authority and pleasure, and if any were assembled together, they must of necessity believe that it was done without his order, he being a captive, it being in their power to deprive him of his life, if any such thing should be ordered by him.

Illustration 16. De Bry, Theodor, ca. 1598. Rescue payment for the release of Atahualpa [engraving]. On: Brevíssima relación de la destruyción de las Indias. Frankfurt, 1598. 3D image on **http://bit.ly/lascasas16.**

Notwithstanding which, they entered into a consultation to have him burnt alive, and a little while after the sentence was agreed upon, but the captain at the insistence of some persons commanded him first to be strangled, then thrown into the fire. The King understanding the sentence of death past upon him, said "Why do you burn me? What fact have I committed deserving death? Did you not promise to set me free for a sum of gold? And did I not give you a far larger quantity than I promised? But if it is your pleasure so to do, send me to your King of Spain" and thus using many words to the same purpose, tending to the confusion and detestation of the Spanish injustice, he was burnt to death. And here let us take into serious consideration the right and title they had to make this war, the captivity, sentence, and execution of this prince, and the conscience wherewith these tyrants have possessed themselves of vast treasures, which they have surreptitiously and fraudulently taken away from this King, and a great many more of the rulers of these kingdoms.

Illustration 17: De Bry, Theodor, ca. 1598. Execution of the Inca Atahualpa [engraving]. On Brevíssima relación de la destruyción de las Indias. Frankfurt, 1598. 3D image on **http://bit.ly/lascasas17.**

But as to the great number of their enormities committed by those who stile themselves Christians in order to the extirpation of this people, I will hear repeat some of them, which in the very beginning were seen by a Franciscan, confirmed by his own letters, and signed with his hand and seal, sending some of them to the Perusian provinces, and others to the Kingdom of Castile. A copy whereof I have in my custody, signed with his hand, as I said before; the contents whereof follow.

"I, Friar Marcos de Xlicia, of the Franciscan order, and prefect of the whole fraternity residing in the Perusian provinces, one of the first among the religious, who arrived with the Spaniards in these parts. I declare with incontrovertible and undeniable testimony, those transactions, which I saw with my own eyes, and particularly such as relate to the usage of the inhabitants of this region. In the first place I was an eye-witness, and am certainly assure, that these Perusians are a people, who transcend all other Indians in meekness, clemency, and love to Spaniards; and I have seen the Indians bestow very liberally on them gold, silver, and jewels, being very serviceable to them many other ways. Nor did the Indians ever betake themselves to their arms in a hostile manner, till by infinite injuries and cruelties they were compelled thereunto: For on the contrary, they gave the Spaniards an amicable and honorable reception in all their towns, and furnished them with provisions, and as many male and female servants as they required.

I can also farther testify, that the Spaniards, without the least provocation on their part, as soon as they entered upon these territories, did burn at the stake their most potent Cacique Ataliba, prince of the whole country, after they had extorted from him above two million of gold, and possessed themselves of his province, without the least opposition: and Cochilimaca, his captain general, who with other rulers, came peaceably into them, followed him by the same fiery trial and death. As also some few days after, Chamba, the ruler of the province of Quito, was burnt without any cause given, or crime laid to his charge. They likewise put Chapera, Prince of the Canaries, to the same death, and in like manner, burnt the feet of Albis, the greatest of all the Quitonian lords, and racked him with other torments to extract from him a discovery of Ataliba's treasure, whereof as appeared after, he was totally ignorant. Thus, they treated Cozopanga, governor of all the provinces of Quito, who being overcome with the entreaties of Sebastian Benalcázar[60], the governors captain, went peaceably to pay them a visit; but because he could not give them as much gold as they demanded, they burnt him with many other Caciques and chief persons of quality. And as I understand, did it with this evil intention, that they might not leave one surviving lord or peer in the whole country."

---

[60] Benalcázar was the conqueror of Nicaragua. He was one of the members of Pizarro's first expedition.

THE EXECUTION OF THE INCA.

*Illustration 18: Greene, A. B., ca 1891. The execution of the Inca. On: The New World Heroes of discovery and conquest. Philadelphia, Pa.: National Publishing Company, P.404, 3D image on **http://bit.ly/lascasas18**.*

"I also affirm that I saw with these eyes of mine the Spaniards for no other reason, but only to gratify their bloody mindedness, cut off the hands, noses, and ears, both of Indians and Indianeses, and that in so many places and parts, that it would be too prolix and tedious to relate them. Nay, I have seen the Spaniards let loose their dogs upon the Indians to bait and tear them in pieces, and such a number of villages burnt by them as cannot well be discover: Farther this is a certain truth, that they snatched babes from the mother's embraces, and taking hold of their arms threw them away as far as they would from them: (a pretty kind of bar-tossing recreation.) They committed many other cruelties, which shook me with terror at the very sight of them and would take up too much time in the relation.

Illustration 19: De Bry, Theodor, ca. 1598. The goal of the Spaniards was that there were no masters left in the whole Land [recorded]. On: Brevíssima relación de la destruyción de las Indias. Frankfurt, 1598. 3D image on http://bit.ly/lascasas19.

I likewise aver, that the Spaniards gathered together as many Indians as filled three houses, to which, for no cause, (or a very inconsiderable one) they set fire, and burnt every one of them: but a presbyter, Ocana by name, chanced to snatch a little baby out of the fire, which being observed by a Spaniard, he tore him out of his arms, and threw him into the midst of the flames, where he was with the rest, soon burnt to ashes, which Spaniard the same day he committed that fact, returning to his quarters, died suddenly by the way, and I advised them not to give him Christian burial.

Furthermore, I saw them send to several Caciques and principal Indians, promising them a protecting passport to travel peaceably and securely to them, who, no sooner came, but they were burnt; two of them before my face, one at Andonia, and the other at Tumbala. Nor could I with all my persuasions and preaching to them prevail so far as to save them from the Fire. And this I do maintain according to God and my own conscience, as far as I could possibly learn, that the inhabitants of Perú never promoted or raised any commotion or rebellion, though as it is manifest to all men, they were afflicted with evil dealings and cruel torments: And they, not without cause, the Spaniards breaking their faith and word, betraying the truth and tyrannically contrary to all law and justice, destroying them and the whole country, inflicting on them great injuries and losses, were more ready to prepare themselves for death, than still to fall at once into such great and irrecoverable miseries.

Nay I do declare, according to Information from the Indians themselves, that there are to this day far greater quantities of gold kept hid and concealed than ever were yet detected or brought to light, which by means of the Spanish injustice and cruelty, they would not then, nor ever will discover so long as they are so barbarously treated, but will rather chose to dye with the herd. Whereat the Lord God is highly offended and the King hath very ill offices done him, for he is hereby defrauded of this region, which was sufficiently able to furnish all Castile with necessaries, the recovery whereof can never be expected without great difficulty and vast Expenses."

Thus far I have acquainted you with the very words of this religious Franciscan, ratified by the Bishop of Mexico, who testified that the said friar Marcos did affirm and maintain what is above-mentioned. Here it is to be observed what this said friar was an eye-witness of; for he travelled up in this country 50 or 100 leagues, for the space of 9 or 10 years, when as yet, few Spaniards had got footing there, but afterward, at the noise of gold to be had there in great plenty, four and five thousand came thither, who spread themselves through those kingdoms and provinces the space of five and six hundred leagues, which they made wholly desolate, committing the same, or greater cruelties than are before recited. In reality, they destroyed from that time to these very days, 1,000 poor souls over than what he gives an account of, and with less fear of God and the King. Nay with less mercy have they destroyed the greatest part of mankind in these kingdoms, above four million, suffering violent death.

A few days after they darted to death with arrows made of reeds a puissant queen, the wife the Inca potentate, who still sways the imperial scepter of that kingdom, whom the Spaniards had a design to take, which instigated him to raise a rebellion, and he still continues a rebel. They seized the queen his consort, and contrary to all law and equity murdered her, as is said before, who was then, as report, big with child, only for this reason, that they might add fresh affliction and grief to her husband. If the particular cruelties and massacres that the Christians in those kingdoms of Perú have committed and are committed today are to be counted, they would undoubtedly be frightful, and so many that everything we have said of the other parties is made to appear and seem little, according to the quantity and severity of them.

OF THE NEW KINGDOM OF GRANADA

http://bit.ly/gran-brief

Many tyrants there were, who set sail from Venezuela, St. Martha, and Cartagena, hastening to the conquest of Perú, Anno Dom. 1539. And many were coming from Perú, endeavored to penetrate into the heart of this country, where they found about three leagues from Cartagena and St. Martha, many admirable provinces and most fruitful land, furnished with an even-tempered or meek-spirited people, as there are in other parts of India. It was very rich in gold and those sorts of precious stones known by the name of emeralds. They gave the name of Granada to this province because the tyrant, who first arrived in these regions[61], was born in the Kingdom of Granada belonging to these parts. Now they that spoiled these provinces with their rapine being wicked, cruel, infamous butchers, and delighting in the effusion of humane blood, having practically experimented the sins and grand enormities perpetrated among the Indians. Upon this account, their diabolical actions are so great, so many in number, and represented so grievously horrid by circumstantial aggravations, that they exceed all the villainies committed by others, nay by themselves in other regions, I will only select and cull out a few out of so great a number which have bene transacted by them within these three years, for my present purpose.

A certain governor, because he that went to commit depredations and spoils in the kingdom of Granada, would not admit him, as a companion in

---

[61] Jiménez de Quesada.

his robberies and cruelties, set up an inquisition, and produced proofs confirmed by great evidence, whereby he palpably lays open, and proves the slaughters and homicides he committed, and persists in to this very day, which were read in the Indian courts of judicature, and are there now recorded.

In this Inquisition the witnesses depose, that when all these kingdoms enjoyed peace and tranquility, the Indians served the Spaniards, and got their living by constant day-labor in tilling and manuring the ground, bringing them much gold, and many gems, particularly emeralds, and what other commodities they could, and possessed, their cities and dominions being divided among the Spaniards, to procure which is the chiefest of their care and pains. These are the proper measures they take to obtain their proposed ends, to wit, heaping and treasuring up of gold and riches. Now when all the Indians were under their accustomed tyranny: a certain tyrant, and chief commander, took the King and lord of the whole country, and detained him captive for six or seven months, demanding of him, without any reason, store of gold and emeralds. The said king, whose name was Bogotá, though fear, promised him a house of gold, hoping, in time, to escape out of his clutches, who thus plagued him, and sent some Indians for gold, who frequently, and at several times, brought him a great quantity of gold, and many jewels. But, because the King did not, according to his promise, bestow upon him an apartment made of pure gold, he must therefore forfeit his life. The tyrant commanded him to be brought to trial before himself, and so they cite and summon to a trial the greatest King in the whole region; and the tyrant pronounced this sentence, that unless he did perform his golden promise he should be exposed to severe torments. They racked, poured boiling soap into his bowels, chained his legs to one post, and fastened his neck to another, two men holding his hands, and so applied the scorching heat of the fire to his feet; the tyrant himself often casting his eye upon him, and threatening him with death, if he did not give him the promised gold; and thus with these kind of horrid torments, the said lord was destroyed; which while they were doing, God being willing to manifest how displeasing these cruelties are to his divine majesty, the whole city, that was the stage on which they were acted, was consumed by fire; and the rest of the captains following his example, destroyed all the lords of that region by fire and faggot.

For fear of egregious cruelties that one of the tyrants did a great gentleman named Daitama, went fleeing to the mountains so much inhumanity of its people. And this is what the Spanish call uprisings and rebellion. Known by the main captain, he sent people to the tyrant whose ferocity the Indians had gone to the mountains. He went to look for them, found a large number of people, and shattered more than five hundred souls, among men, women, and children (because they didn't forgive any gender). Witnesses still say that Daitama himself had brought four or five thousand castilians to the tyrant before his people were killed.

Once it fell out, that many Indians addressed themselves to the Spaniards with all humility and simplicity, as they use to do, who thinking themselves safe and secure, behold the captain comes into the city, where they were to do their work, and commands all these Indians, sleeping and taking their rest, after supper, being wearied with the heavy drudgery of the day, to be slain by the sword. This stratagem he put in practice, to make a greater impression of fear on all the minds of the inhabitants.

Another time a certain captain commanded the Spaniards to declare upon oath, how many Caciques and Indians every individual person had in his family at home. Then, the Spaniards were told to lead then to a public place, where they lost their heads; so about, 400 or 500 souls perished. Witnesses depose this of a particular tyrant, that by beating, cutting off the hands and noses of many women as well as men, and destroying several persons in great numbers, he exercised horrid cruelties.

Then one of the captains sent this bloody tyrant into the province of Bogotá, to inquire who succeeded that prince there, whom he so barbarously and inhumanely murder, who traveling many leagues in this country, took as many Indians as he could get, some of which, because they did not tell him who was successor of this deceased Prince, had their hands cut off, and others were exposed to hunger- starved curs, to be devoured by them, and as many of them perished miserably. Another time about the fourth watch, early in the morning he fell upon several Caciques, noblemen and other Indians, who looked upon themselves to be safe enough, (for they had their faith and security given, that none of them should receive any damage or injury) relying upon this, they left the mountains their lurking places, without any suspicion or fear, and returned to their cities, but he seized on them all, and commanding them to extend their hands on the ground, cut them off with his own sword, saying, that he punished them after this manner, because they would not inform him what lord it was, that succeeded in that kingdom.

Another time, the Indians of one of these provinces, perceiving that four or five of their governors were sent to the other world in a fiery vehicle or chariot, being terrified therewith, took to the mountains for sanctuary, there being 4000 or 5000 in number, as told by witnesses. The aforesaid captain sends a tyrant, crueler than any of the rest after them. The Spaniards ascend the mountains by force (for the Indians were naked and unarmed) proclaiming peace, if they would desist and lay down their arms, which the Indians no sooner heard, but quitted their childish weapons; and this was no sooner done but this sanguinary Spaniard sent some to possess themselves of the fortifications, and they being secure, to attack the Indians. Thus they, like wolves and lions, did rush upon this flock of sheep, and were so tired with slaughter, that they were forced to desist for a while and take breath, which done, the captain commands them to fall to it again at the same bloody rate, and precipitate all that survived the butchery, from the top of the mountain, which was of a prodigious height; and that was performed accordingly. And the witnesses farther declare upon oath, that they saw the bodies of about seven hundred Indians falling from the mount at one time, like a cloud obscuring the air, who were all broken to pieces.

Illustration 20: De Bry, Theodor, ca. 1598. Indian mutilation [engraving]. On: Brevíssima relación de la destruyción de las Indias. Frankfurt, 1598. 3D image on **http://bit.ly/lascasas20.**

Again, this same tyrant went to a certain town called Cota and took many Indians and made the dogs tear apart fifteen or twenty lords and principals. He cut many hands of women and men, tied them on some ropes, hung them on a stick to the long, because the other Indians saw what he had done to them, in which there would be seventy pairs of hands, and cut many noses to women and children.

The witnesses farther depose, that the cruelties and great slaughters committed in the aforesaid new kingdom of Granada, by this captain, and other tyrants, the destroyers of mankind, who accompany him, and have power still given them by him to exercise the same, are such and so heinous, that if his Majesty does not opportunely apply some remedy, for the redress and prevention of such mischiefs for the future, (since the Indians are daily slaughtered to accumulate and enrich themselves with gold, which the inhabitants have been so robbed of, that they are now grown bare, for what they had, they have disposed to the Spaniards already) this kingdom will soon decay and be made desolate, and consequently the land being destitute of

Indians, who should manure it, will lie fallow and uncultivated.

And here is to be noted, how pestilential and inhumane the cruelty of these tyrants hath been, and how violently exercised, when as in two or three years space, they were all slain, and the country wholly desolate and deserted, as those that have been eye-witnesses can testified; they having acted like merciless men, not having the fear of God and the King before their eyes, but by the instigation of the devil; so that it may well be said and affirmed, not one person will be left alive, unless his Majesty does retard, and put a stop to the full career of their cruelties, which I am very apt to believe, for I have seen with these very eyes of mine, many kingdoms laid waste and depopulated in a small time.

There are other stately provinces on the confines of the new kingdom of Granada, as Popayan and Cali, together with three or four more above five hundred leagues in length, which they destroyed, in the same manner, as they have done other places, and laid them absolutely waste by the aforementioned slaughters, who were very populous, and the soil very fruitful. They who came among us from those regions report, that nothing can be more deplorable or worthy of pity and commiseration, then to behold such large and great cities totally ruined, and entombed in their own ashes, and that in a city adorned with 1,000 and 2,000 neighbors, there are hardly now to be seen 50 standing, the rest being utterly demolished, or consumed and levelled to the ground by fire and in some parts regions of 100 leagues in length, (containing spacious cities) are found absolutely destroyed and consumed by fire.

Finally, many great tyrants who came out of the Perusian kingdoms by the Quitonians travelled to the said new kingdom of Granada, Popayán, and Cali. Other tyrants took off from the Cartagena and Urabá regions and directed their course to Quito. They all joined themselves in an entire body and wholly depopulated that region for the space of 600 leagues and upward, with the loss of a prodigious number of poor souls; nor as yet do they treat the small remnant of so great and innocent a people.

And because the rule I said at the beginning is true, that the tyranny, violence, and injustices of the Spaniards against the victims of meekness in crudeness, inhumanity and evil were always growing. What is now done in the various provinces, among other things worthy of all fire and torment, is the following. After the deaths and ravages of the wars the people arrived in the horrible serfdom, and the devils included one 200 and another 300 Indians. A commander calls one hundred Indians before him. When they arrive (like lambs), cut off the heads of 30 or 40 of them and say to the others "I will do the same if you do not serve me well or if you go without my license."

I desire therefore that the readers who have or shall peruse these passages, would please seriously to consider whether or not, such barbarous, cruel and inhumane acts as these do not transcend and exceed all the impiety and tyranny, which can enter into the thoughts or imagination of man, and whether these Spaniards deserve not the name of devils. For which of these two things is more eligible or desirable whether the Indians should be delivered up to the devils themselves to be tormented or the Spaniards? That is still a question.

Nor can I here omit one piece of villany, (whether it ought to be postponed or come behind the cruelty of brute animals, that I leave to decision). The Spaniards who are conversant among the Indians bred up curst curs, who are so well instructed and taught that they at first sight, fly upon the inhabitants tearing them limb by limb, and so presently devour them. Now let all persons whether Christians or not consider, if ever such a thing as this reached the ears of any man, they carry these dogs with them as companions where ever they go, and kill the fettered Indians in multitudes like hogs for their food; thus sharing with them in the butchery. Nay they frequently call one to the other, saying, "lend me the fourth part of one of your slaves to feed my dogs, and when I kill one, I will repay you," as if they had only borrowed a quarter of a hog or sheep. Others, when they go a hunting early in the morning, upon their return, if you ask them what sport had you today at the game? They will answer, "enough, enough, for my dogs have killed and worried 15 or 20 Indian vassals." Now all these things are plainly proved upon those inquisitions and examinations made by one tyrant against another. What I beseech you, can be more horrid or barbarous?

But I will desist from writing any longer at this time, till some Messenger brings an account of greater and blacker Impieties (if greater can be committed) or else till we come to behold them again, as we have done for the space of forty-two years with our own Eyes. I will only make this small addition to what I have said that the Spaniards, from the beginning of their first entrance upon America to this present day, were no more solicitous of promoting the preaching of the gospel of Christ to these nations, then if they had been dogs or beasts, but which is worst of all, they expressly prohibited their addresses to the religious, laying many heavy impositions upon them, daily afflicting and persecuting them, that they might not have so much time and leisure at their own disposal, as to attend their preaching and divine service; for they looked upon that to be an impediment to their getting gold, and raking up riches which their avarice stimulated them so boundlessly to prosecute. Nor do they understand any more of a God, whether he be made of wood, brass or clay, then they did above a hundred years ago, New Spain only exempted, which is a small part of America, and was visited and instructed by the religious. Thus, they did formerly and still do perish without true faith, or the knowledge and benefit of our religious sacraments.

I, Friar Bartolomé de las Casas, or Casaus, of the order of St. Dominic, who through the mercy of God arrived at the Spanish Court, Cordially wishing the expulsion of hell or these hellish acts out of the Indies; fearing least those souls redeemed by the precious blood of Christ, should perish eternally, but heartily desiring that they may acknowledge their Creator and be saved; as also for the care and compassion that I ever had for my native country Castile, dreading least God should destroy it for the many sins committed by the natives her children, against faith, honor and their neighbors: I have at length upon the request of some persons of great quality in this court, who are fervently zealous of the honor of God, and moved with pity at the calamities and afflictions of their neighbors (though I long since proposed it within myself, and resolved to accomplish it, but could not, being distracted with the avocations of multiplicity of constant business and employment, have leisure to effect it).

I say I have at length finished this treatise and summary at Valencia, December 8, Ann. Dom. 1542, when these are at the height, and utmost degree of executing violence, oppressions, tyranny, desolations, torments, and calamities in all the aforesaid regions, inhabited by the Spaniards (though they are crueler in some places than other). Mexico with its confines were more favorably treated than the rest of the provinces. And indeed, no man durst openly and publicly do any injury to the inhabitants; for there some justice, (which is nowhere else in India) though very little is done and practiced; yet they are grievously oppressed with intolerable taxes. But, I do really believe, and am fully persuaded that our Sovereign Lord Charles the Fifth, Emperor and King of Spain, our Lord and Prince, who begins to be sensible of the wickedness and treacheries, which have been, and still are committed against this miserable nation, and distressed countries contrary to the will and pleasure of God, as well as His Majesties that he will in time, (for hitherto the truth hath been concealed and kept from his knowledge, with as great craft, as fraud and malice) totally extirpate and root up all these evils and mischiefs, and apply such proper medicines as may purge the morbific and peccant humours in the politic body of this New World, committed to his care and government as a lover and promoter of peace and tranquility. God preserve and bless him with renown and a happy life in his imperial state, and prosper him in all his attempts, that he may remedy the distempers of the Christian church, and crown him at last with eternal felicity, Amen.

After I had published this treatise, certain laws and constitutions, enacted by his Majesty then at Barcelona in the month of December, Ann. Dom. 1542, promulgated and published the year ensuing in the City of Madrid, whereby it is provided, (as the present necessities require) that a period be put to such great enormities and sins, as were committed against God and our neighbors, and tended to the utter ruine and perdition of this New World. These laws were published by his Majesties order, several persons of highest authority, counselors, learned, and conscientious men, being assembled together for that purpose, and many debates made at Valladolid about this weighty affair, at length by the unanimous consent and advice of all those who had committed their opinions to writing, they were made public who traced more closely therein the laws of Christ and Christianity, and were judged persons pure, free from and innocent of that stain and blemish of depriving the Indians of their treasures by theft and rapine, which riches had contaminated and sullied the hands, but much more the souls of those who were enslaved by those heaps of wealth and covetousness, now this obstinate and hot pursuit after wealth was the original of all those evils committed without the least remorse or check of conscience.

These laws being thus promulgated, the courtiers who promoted these tyrants, took care that several copies should be transcribed, (though they were extremely afflicted to see, that there were no farther hopes or means to promote the former depredations and extortions by the tyranny aforesaid) and sent them to several Indian provinces. They, who took upon them the trouble and care of extirpating, and oppressing by different ways of cruelty, as they never observed any method or order, but behaved themselves most inordinately and irregularly, having perused these diplomats or constitutions, before the new made judges, appointed to put them in execution, could arrive or be landed, they by the assistance of those (as 'tis credibly rumor, nor is it repugnant to truth) who hitherto favored their criminal and violent actions, knowing well that these laws and proclamations must necessarily take effect, began to grow mutinous, and rebel, and when the judges were landed, who were to execute these mandates, laying aside all manner of love and fear of god, were so audacious as to contemn and set at nought all the reverence and obedience due to their King, and so became traitors, demeaning themselves like blood-thirsty tyrants, destitute and void of all humanity.

More particularly this appeared in the Perusian kingdoms, where Ann. Dom. 1542, they acted such horrid and stupendous enormities, that the like was never known or heard in America, or throughout the whole world before that time: Nor were they only practiced upon the Indians, who were mostly destroyed, but upon themselves also, God permitting them by his just judgment to be their own executioners, and sheath their swords in one another's bowels. in like manner the other parts of this new world being moved by the example of these rebels, refused to yield obedience to those laws. The rest pretending to petition his majesty turn rebellious themselves; for they would not voluntarily resign those estates, goods and chattels they have already usurped, nor willingly manumit those Indians, who were doomed to be their slaves, during life; and where they restrained the murdering sword from doing execution, they oppressed them gradually with personal vassalage, unjust and intolerable burthens; which his Majesty could not possibly hitherto avert or hinder, because they are all universally, some publicly and openly, others clancularly and secretly, so naturally addicted to rob, thieve and steal; and thus under pretext of serving the king, they dishonor God, and defraud his Imperial Majesty.

***

Here the author having finished the matter of fact in this compendious history, for confirmation of what he has here written, quotes a tedious and imperfect epistle (as he styles it) beginning and ending anonymous withal, containing the cruelties committed by the Spaniards, the same in effect as our author has aforementioned. Now in regard that I judge such reiterated cruelties and repeated barbarisms are offensive to the reader, he having sailed already too long, and too far in an ocean of innocent Indian blood. I have omitted all but two or three stories not taken notice of by the author. One of the tyrants, (who followed the steps of John Ampudia, a notorious villain) gave way to a great slaughter of sheep the chief food and support of the Spaniards as well as Indians, permitting them to kill two or three hundred at a time, only for their brains, fat, or suet, whose flesh was then altogether useless, and not fit to be eaten; but many Indians, the Spaniards friends and confederates followed them, desiring they might have the hearts to feed upon, whereupon they butchered a great many of them, for this only reason, because they would not eat the other parts of the body. Two of their gang in the province of Perú killed twenty-five sheep, who were sold among the Spaniards for twenty-five castelians, merely to get the fat and brains out of them. Thus, the frequent and extraordinary slaughter of their sheep above a hundred thousand head of cattle were destroyed. And upon this Account the region was reduced to great penury and want, and at length perished with hunger. Nay the Province of Quito, which abounded with corn beyond expression, by such proceedings as these, was brought to that extremity that a sextarie or small measure or wheat was sold for ten castelians, and a sheep at as dear a rate.

This captain taking leave of Quito was followed by a poor Indianess with loud cries and clamors, begging and beseeching him not to carry away her husband; for she had the charge of three children, and could not possibly supply them with victuals, but they must inevitably dye with hunger, and though the captain repulsed her with an angry brow at the first; yet she approached him a second time with repeated cries, saying, that her children must perish for want of food; but finding the captain inexorable and altogether unmoved with her complaints, and her husband not restor, through a piquant necessity wedded to despair; she cut off the heads of her children with sharp stones, and so dispatched them into the other world.

Then he proceeded farther to another city, and sent some Spaniards that very night, to take the Indians of the city of Tulilicui, who next day brought with them above a hundred persons; some of which (whom he looked upon to be able to carry burthens) he reserved for his own and his soldiers service, and other were chained, and perished in their Fetters: but the little Infants he gave to the Cacique of Tulilicui, above said to be eaten up and devoured, whose skins are stuffed with ashes and hung up in his house to be seen at this very day. And in the close of this letter he shuts up all with these words, 'tis here very remarkable and never to be forgotten, that this tyrant (being not ignorant of the mischiefs and enormities executed by him) boastingly said of himself, "they who shall travel in these countries fifty years hence, and hear the things related of me, will have cause to say or declare, that never such a tyrant as I am marched through these regions, and committed the like enormities."

Now not to quit the stage without one comical scene or action whereon such cruelties have been lively personated, give me leave to acquaint you with a comical piece of grammatical learning in a reverend religioso of these parts, sent thither to convert the West-Indies pagans, which the author mentions among his reasons and replications, and all these I pass by as immaterial to our purpose, many of them being repeated in the narrative before.

The weight and burthen of initiating the Indians into the Christian faith lay solely on the Spaniards at first; and therefore Joannes Colmenero in Santa Martha, a fantastic, ignorant, and foppish fellow, was under examination before us (and he had one of the most spacious cities committed to his charge as well as the care and cure of the souls of the inhabitants) whether he understood how to cross-over himself with the sign of the cross against the wicked and impious, and being interrogated what he taught, and how he instructed the Indians, whose souls were entrusted to his care and conduct; he returned this answer, That if he damned them to the devil and furies of hell, it was sufficient to retrieve them, if he pronounced these words, per signin sanctin cruces. A fellow fitter to be a hog herd than a shepherd of souls.

This deep, bloody American tragedy is now concluded, and my pen choked up with Indian blood and gore. I have no more to say, but pronounce the epilogue made by the author, and leave the reader to judge whether it deserves a plaudite.

The Spaniards first set sail to America, not for the honor of God, or as persons moved and merited thereunto by servant zeal to the true faith, nor to promote the salvation of their neighbors, nor to serve the King, as they falsely boast and pretend to do, but in truth, only stimulated and goaded on by insatiable avarice and ambition, that they might forever domineer, command, and tyrannize over the West-Indians, whose kingdoms they hoped to divide and distribute among themselves. Which to deal candidly in no more or less intentionally, than by all these indirect ways to disappoint and expel the Kings of Castile out of those dominions and territories, that they themselves having usurped the Supreme and Regal Empire, might first challenge it as their right, and then possess and enjoy it.

FINIS.

Made in the USA
San Bernardino, CA
17 June 2020

73548669R00063